INSPIRATIONAL
WOMEN

D0932675

INSPIRATIONAL WOMEN

Interviews with 12 women
who encourage, enlighten and entertain

NIKKI HENRIQUES

GRAPEVINE

First published 1988

British Library Cataloguing in Publication Data

Henriques, Nikki
Inspirational women.
1. Great Britain. Women — Biographies
I. Title
920.72'0941

ISBN 0-7225-1538-3

*Grapevine is an imprint of the Thorsons Publishing Group,
Wellingborough, Northamptonshire, NN8 2RQ, England*

Printed in Great Britain by Biddles Limited,
Guildford, Surrey, England

3 5 7 9 10 8 6 4 2

For Annie
always my friend and sometimes my inspiration.

Contents

Acknowledgements 9
Introduction 11

Shirley Conran 15
Cleo Laine 25
Linda Bellos 39
Carole Tongue 53
Jane Lapotaire 69
Liz Hodges 91
Jenny Hilton 107
Julia Neuberger 121
Bridget Riley 137
Mikki Doyle 145
Mary Stott 165
Miriam Karlin 177

Acknowledgements

My deepest thanks go to the truly inspirational women who made time in their busy schedules to be interviewed. I feel privileged and enriched to have spent time with (alphabetically) Linda Bellos, Mikki Doyle, Jenny Hilton, Liz Hodges, Miriam Karlin, Cleo Laine, Jane Lapotaire, Julia Neuberger, Bridget Riley, Mary Stott and Carole Tongue. You skilfully dispelled my anxiety and were all extremely welcoming of my intrusion into your privacy.

I would also like to thank Fay Franklin, Marj Nelson and Judith Smallwood at Thorsons for allowing me to develop their original idea; Anne Dickson for her insight and contribution at some of the interviews, and many of the questions as well as the synopsis; Kate Allen for her editorial support and Elaine Thompson for her picture research.

I hope many people will enjoy the fruits of our collective labours.

NH

Introduction

When I began compiling this book I felt isolated, dejected and depressed. My personal campaign for justice and equality of opportunity for everyone seemed inappropriate and completely out of step with the overtly materialistic and highly competitive First World culture in which I live and work.

Meeting and talking with these remarkable women has had a tremendous impact on my spiritual and emotional strength. In their very different ways they have taught me about the importance of commitment, honesty, channelling of energy, and expression of passion. Their clarity, inner strength and quiet achievement is inspirational.

Each woman is successful in her particular profession, and in her own right. They talk about their motivation, inspiration, hopes and triumphs, how they manage criticism, compromise, sacrifice, failure, vulnerability, how they express their anger, and how they relax and re-charge.

I never sought to achieve a political balance in my choice of interviewees. Those who agreed to be interviewed and expressed a political point of view coincidentally happen to be left rather than right wing. I chose to interview a mixture of women who are already an inspiration to others, as well as lesser known personalities, in the hope that their practical, often moving and amusing accounts of their lives will sound echoes in ordinary women. Perhaps, like me, you'll feel less isolated and alone in what seems, from time to time, to be a very hostile world.

Compiling the book has taught me to reflect upon and honour the spirit that is female, and given me the strength to battle against adversity in my own individual way. It's made me realize the

importance of acknowledging and appreciating the unique
contribution women have to make in the development and
evolution of a happier, healthier, more equal and just
society.

Nikki Henriques
London,
December 1987

Shirley Conran. Reproduced courtesy of Camera Press.

Shirley Conran

Writer

Shirley Conran has always been a very special inspiration to me. We have a lot in common because we share the same birth date. I don't see enough of her now, but I remember when I was aspiring to be a journalist she taught me a great deal about the job, and in particular showed me how important it was to be honourable to one's contacts in what has sadly become a dishonourable profession, how to research a subject thoroughly and write decent copy. I've known Shirley during some of her lowest moments and been astonished at the seemingly endless energy, courage and determination she employs in turning any adverse situation right around to make it work for her benefit. She is one of the kindest, most resourceful women I've ever met and, I think, a real professional. Having chased her round the world by telephone while she promoted her latest book, I finally caught up with her on her return home to Monte Carlo.

Who has inspired you, Shirley? Who would you wish to emulate?

I think I can truthfully say no one person has inspired me, although at times, for different reasons, I've wanted to emulate Grace Darling's bravery and selflessness, and Elizabeth I of England, because I think she guided the country through a period of incredible prosperity so deftly.

Carol, a battered wife I know, dragged herself and her children away from her husband, and survived and raised her children by learning to paint and decorate houses. Now she has a very successful specialist interior painting and decorating business.

She's an inspiration because she got out from under and succeeded against all the odds. I know how difficult it must have been for her, because I know what it's like to be thumped. I had a violent father, but unless you've had that experience you can't possibly understand how badly it affects you. It leaves you greatly disadvantaged with no feeling of self-worth at all.

Did you set yourself goals?

Not really. I didn't plan my life at all. I left school at 14 and I used to think that lacking a university education was a bad thing, but I'm beginning to think it's not such a great disadvantage after all, because I think a university education does little more than teach you how to spout second-hand opinions and not to think for yourself.

I never decided to have a career. No one taught me how to write because nobody thought I would want to do it.

My real writing career didn't start till I was 45. I'm now 55. It started well after my stint as a Fleet Street editor, and well after *Superwoman*, which I wrote when I was 42. I think one of the mistakes I made was taking the first job that came along. I should have been less anxious and a bit more choosy.

Over the years I suppose I've smashed my way through a good many barriers I never knew existed, without knowing what I was doing or how I did it. Once, during my activities campaigning for legislation against sex discrimination, a bunch of MPs sympathetic to the cause invited me to lunch at the House of Commons to give me useful books and information on how Parliament worked. I turned up for the lunch but there were no books. They told me I'd be much more successful operating in the way I did, not really knowing what I was up against.

I think that Audrey Slaughter did that when she launched *Over 21*. I'm sure if she'd had an inkling of what she was getting herself into she wouldn't have done it. Yet in the end she built up a hugely successful magazine, and when she left she took with her a 14,000 per cent profit on her original financial investment.

When you risk everything in that way, it must be wonderful to have have a reliable partner, someone to talk to, to stand by you in the hard times, when the going gets tough.

Was encouragement for what you did forthcoming?

I got the greatest encouragement and support from my early bosses. Gordon McKenzie was one; he gave me my first chance in Fleet Street as home editor of the *Daily Mail*. Then there was E. A. Robinson, a extremely skilful and well-respected *Daily Mail* sub-editor. He had to put up with my copy, and taught me a great deal.

I remember we had a famous Australian writer seconded to our 'Femail' team. Mr Robinson came in one day and said 'We don't like your piece. You've got 17 minutes to write another one.' My Australian colleague jumped up and down saying we couldn't possibly produce anything in that time. I waited until she'd finished, then said 'Now we've got only 13 minutes, so let's get on and do something.'

George Seddon was a great source of encouragement when I was fashion editor of the *Observer*. He was the person who gave me confidence in my own personality and taught me to be myself. I think the way he did it was to giggle a lot at my jokes and then go and put them in that week's newspaper. I think he saw my life as his own personal comic strip.

Caroline Mackinlay was another very supportive colleague. She also worked on the *Observer*. I was doing a lot of promotional events for the paper. I had organized an exhibition at Heals which had broken all records for daily attendance. The editor of the newspaper asked to see me, and I thought he would pat me on the back, give me a bunch of daisies and say, 'Well done!' Instead he fired me. Well, I wasn't exactly fired, I was offered the option of leaving or staying on as either design or cookery editor.

I reeled back to my office, which in those days wasn't much bigger than a lavatory, and my secretary, Caroline Baker (now a top fashion editor) was there. She's so businesslike and professional I think she ought to be running the country! Anyway, Caroline Baker had been told not to take any more instructions from me, but the first thing Caroline Mackinlay did was tell Caroline Baker to continue to work with me. We all got on very well together, so I stayed.

My current encouragement and support comes mainly from my fellow bestselling writers such as Jackie Collins, Barbara Taylor Bradford and Judith Krantz. The great thing is, none of us gossip about each other or are at all envious of each other. We're all very supportive and encourage each other as much as we can.

How have your family, friends, partner reacted to your success?

Most of the time they ignore it. Except for *Lace* which I know they all went out and bought immediately because it's auto-biographical. I suspect none of them have read any of the others I've written.

My partner, Mike, is very supportive. He's the first man in my life who's taken any interest in my work, and, apart from my mother, he's the only person who remembers everyone who's ever done me down. Not only is he my partner, but my best friend.

What do you regard as your greatest success?

My sons, Jasper and Sebastian. Especially having Jasper by natural childbirth. I got out of hand for about 30 seconds but responded well to my gynaecologist's sergeant-major approach. I have to say that giving birth to Jasper was the greatest physical experience of my life. I enjoyed every moment of it, even the labour, and from birth he's been a most considerate son. I even watched television during the early stages of labour, and the contractions only came on during the commercial breaks!

He's very intuitive, knows just how to make you feel tremendous, and is a water diviner.

Sebastian is equally wonderful, but in a different way. He's very good at practical solutions. If you've got a problem and go to him for help, he'll solve your problem, but he won't give you much sympathy.

I think my books are a combination of those approaches. The pills are sugar-coated but the message is there just the same.

What about making money?

If you asked me whether I prefer being rich or poor, I prefer being rich. Being poor means you have very few choices in life. Having money means you have many more choices. I want everyone to have as much choice as possible. I get hundreds of requests for money and I give away a great deal; a certain sum is set aside in a special budget and is distributed annually but I never give to anyone who asks.

How do you deal with criticism?

I was totally unprepared for the success of *Superwoman*. I was also totally unprepared for the blast of malice that accompanied its success.

I've discovered the best way of dealing with criticism is not to open my post, or the door, or answer my telephone to anyone. Any nasty notices and letters are thrown away by Mike, so I never get to see them. I thrive on positive criticism. My sons are my best critics, along with George Seddon, Bruce Chatwin, Michael Korda, my US editor, and my agent, Morton Janklow. They all criticize my work constructively and I appreciate their input enormously.

Have you had to compromise in any way because you are a woman?

Only over the opposite sex. I've been married three times, but the trouble is I always put my savings into the marriage and when it breaks up, I'm broke.

Do you find it difficult to make yourself a top priority?

Not as far as my work is concerned. I have high work standards and what many people think is an exasperating tendency to do something over and over again, until I get it exactly right.

How do you nurture yourself?

I suffer from low blood pressure which means that frequently I have to lie flat for short periods during the day. I've found the most convenient way of doing this is to have a bath, with the bathroom darkened, for a quarter of an hour alone. It's extremely important to be alone when I'm re-charging my batteries.

I also have to eat a little and often; if I don't have a proper breakfast, by 11 a.m., I go into 'executive slump'.

Have you experienced failure?

I think being sacked must constitute failure to some degree, but my personal definition of failure is not trying. If you never try anything, you'll never succeed. I always talk openly about my failure. I've never locked anything away because I think people will always find out about it anyway.

Is it difficult managing a private and public life?

It's very difficult separating my private and public life because I enjoy my work so much. I can't stand the publicity that accompanies a book launch, but it's part of the job, so I have to put up with it; in particular, I hate being photographed — oh, I hate it *all*!

What have been your highest and lowest moments?

Having my children rank as my highest moments. My lowest moments concern treachery, especially when it involves someone I thought was a close friend. I find it very difficult coping with people who want to jack up their careers by deliberately sabotaging mine. There are a lot of people around who say that they've written my books — especially the sex scenes — just to get attention, and of course they succeed. I've often thought it would be a good idea to hire the Albert Hall and invite them all along to fight it out for themselves. After two time-consuming legal battles (which I won) I decided to ignore them.

When do you feel most vulnerable?

When I'm tired. That's when I handle everything least well; I'm irritable and snap. I try to manage my vulnerability by doing deep breathing yoga exercises as soon as I begin to feel rattled. That seems to do the trick.

Who or what gives you strength to cope in your lowest moments?

Again, Mike, Jasper and Sebastian, my friends (I have some very good women friends), and my mother.

I remember once, when I was ill and out of work in London, she made the two-hour train journey from her home in Portsmouth to London just to sit and hold my hand while I paid my bills, knowing each cheque got me deeper into debt. She didn't say anything, it was just having her sympathetic and understanding spirit close by me that gave me the strength to cope.

How do you express and manage your anger?

In a most regrettable way. I internalize everything. Because of the kind of father I had, it was never possible to express my anger. So now I bottle it all up and get very resentful, which is supposed to give you cancer.

Distractions help. It was great when I could ski because there's nothing like skiing for concentrating the mind. It's such a dangerous sport, you can't focus on anything else while hurtling down a mountainside, but I bust my shoulders a few years ago and can't ski anymore.

What makes you laugh?

Happy family moments and witty people like Mike and George Seddon. It sounds odd I know, but I'm happiest when I'm being made to laugh at myself. I also love making people laugh myself.

Of what are you most proud?

Of having survived.

Do you have a sense of your own spirituality?

I'm not sure what that means. But my intuition might be seen as an element of my spirituality although mine isn't as strong as Jasper's. But my birth sign is Virgo, so I believe that if you die, you are recycled into the earth, and that the world was created by some amazing natural force. When you compare our pathetic human efforts at creation to the logarithmic spiral of a snail shell or the structure of a sunflower, you know it wasn't man that did it. We can certainly create useful ways to self-destruct effectively, but we're not clever enough to create something as geometrically perfect as a flower. I believe in the great Gardener in the sky.

What lessons have your learned?

I'm extremely gullible. As I try to be truthful and reliable, I expect everyone else to be truthful and reliable and I've had to learn they are *not*, which makes life very difficult.

Never believe what people say, what you are taught or what you read. It makes you too vulnerable. I once advised a group of bored 18-year-olds in a prize-giving address to check out for themselves everything they'd been told and taught. They were delighted; I was telling them to decide for themselves and form their own opinions.

Do you have a personal vision?

I'm not sure if this answers your question, but I want to go on writing books that women find useful; my special subject is female self-confidence — how you lose it and how to find it again, encourage it and keep it.

Cleo Laine.

Cleo Laine OBE

Vocalist

*I travelled northwards into the Buckinghamshire countryside to
meet Cleo Laine. That day she was babysitting her two-year-old
granddaughter, who was asleep upstairs. I shook hands briefly
with her husband, John Dankworth, who discreetly disappeared
to another part of the house, and we sat in the huge vicarage living
room, and with the occasional musical interruption, drank tea
and talked. As we chatted, I discovered we had something in
common. We are both children of racially mixed marriages. My
father was West Indian and my mother English, and she too ran
a boarding house. Being able to share that information was very
important for me. But I began by asking who'd been the greatest
influence in her life.*

At first, when you wrote and asked me who I've admired over
the years, I couldn't think of anybody. Stupid really, because
everyone's been influenced or had mentors at some time during
their lives. So, thinking back carefully, my first and biggest
influence was my mother. She was the first person to tip me
towards what I'm doing today.

She wasn't one of those awful, very pushy stage mums, but
she was certainly ambitious for her son and two daughters. All
three of us were put through dancing and singing classes and
my brother had violin lessons. My father was a very good singer,
so our household was musical in every way and I think the music
lessons were my mother's way of putting the idea in our minds
that the only way we would be able to better ourselves and get
out of the place where we were brought up, was to become
musicians.

We lived in Southall, Middlesex. My father was black and my mother white. You don't realize it at the time, you accept your mother and don't think of her as being different from anyone else. It's only later on in life you realize how heroic those women were in the 1920s and 1930s. In those days, depending on where they lived and their standing in society, it was pretty tough for white women with black husbands. My mother's society was working class and I can remember her chasing people with a broom when anything unkind was said about her children. She looked after us like a mother hen and I have a feeling it was because of people's negative attitudes towards us at the time. I think it's less important today; people accept mixed marriages more easily; although there are still the odd ones who will always have a go.

My mother was very important to me. I can't ever remember feeling deprived in any way, but it was a hard-working household. She ran a boarding house, worked very hard and gave us a lot of attention. She wasn't as musical as my father but she put us on the right path musically, and that made her even more impressive.

Although he never made it professionally, my father was very musical and helped us a great deal. He was a busker and sang in the streets, but I didn't know this until I was 15 or 16. I was going out with a young man, and when I introduced him to my father and he said, 'Oh! I gave him a penny at Waterloo station the other day!' I was so embarrassed. Then I remembered seeing my father counting pennies on the kitchen table and it all tied in.

When did you decide you were going to become a singer?

I never really had any other thought in my head but going on stage; acting, dancing, anything. My mother encouraged me all the time. As I said, she wasn't a pushy stage mum but she took us to any opening or audition she heard of or thought about. My sister was a very good dancer, but, of the three of us, my brother was the pretty, handsome one, her favourite and she took him everywhere. I was a bit too young I know, but I remember auditioning for ENSA. I never, ever succeeded at auditions.

After my mother, film heroines were very important to me — musical films of course. I would sit in the dark watching Judy Garland, Lena Horne; the marvellous, magnificent tap-dancers like Eleanor Powell, Ann Miller. It was a huge cross-section of artists and talent, and I guess that's what has made me such an eclectic singer, in that I like Deanna Durbin and Lena Horne, as well as Shirley Temple. It amazes everyone; they just can't understand why I should like Shirley Temple at all, but she had curls and so did I, and my mother dressed me like her. She was cute, too, when she sang and, anyway, I've always had a kind of 'quirky' ear. It's not quirky to me, but the songs and artists I like, other people generally don't. I liked the songs that other people thought were uncommercial, I guess. Although I never thought of myself as a jazz singer, I was a good candidate and that's how I veered.

I started listening to jazz on the radio, Jazz Club and so on. That's when I first heard John Dankworth who, after my mother and film heroes and heroines, was the next major influence in my life. I never thought I would ever work for him. In the meantime, I continued unsuccessfully auditioning for various bands, entering talent competitions and never winning. So I began to think there must be something very strange about the way I was singing.

It must have been very difficult being rejected over and over again

I didn't mind too much because I considered singing my hobby. I never thought, 'Why am I doing this? Why do I carry on? I'll give myself another year or two then give up.' I never thought that way, I just like singing. I was happy to sing for anyone at any time. I never found it daunting. I never had any doubt at all in my mind that one day I would be successful. I just had to keep on going. As my father used to say as he religiously did the pools each week, 'If you don't put your cross on it you'll never win,' and occasionally he won a little bit. The same motivation was behind me going to all those auditions: if you don't do them, how the hell are you going to win?

I say singing was a hobby because, although my mother wanted us to get into show business, she was wise enough to know that was lucky break stuff. She knew you needed a good back-up profession as well. My sister was a furrier, I was a hairdresser and my brother was a draughtsman.

I started my working life as an apprentice hairdresser, which was really slaving. I was just a skivvy, washing floors and towels, occasionally holding things for the stylist and all for 7s 6d a week! Eventually I left and got a job in a combination hairdresser/

millinery shop. After that I was a librarian, which suited me
because I was pretty lazy but I read a lot. After that I worked in
a pawn shop. I jumped from job to job knowing none of them
were really suitable.

I then got married and had my son, Stuart. That marriage lasted
about eight years. Towards the end of the eighth year I realized
it wasn't going to work.

My big break came when I took a singing job in Southall and
the bass player with the band liked the way I sang. He said he
would try and get me more work. He got me an interview with
a London agent who saw me but wasn't particularly interested.
I think just to get rid of me more than anything else, he said 'I
only have one person on my books who needs a singer. If you'd
like to go down to Jazz Club 41 (just off old Compton Street) John
Dankworth is there. Go and sing for him and see if he likes you.
He knew very well John was a specialist jazz musician and I'm
sure he thought there was no hope for me, but I went anyway.

John was there with his pianist, Bill Le Sage. I sang three songs
for him and he said, 'I can't hire you at the moment because I'm
in a co-operative band, so will you sing tonight in the club so
that the other musicians in the band can hear you?' In retrospect
I think he just wanted a cheap singer! So even though I'd never

John Dankworth.

sung in a jazz club before, and certainly not with musicians of that calibre, I said I'd do it.

John and Bill Le Sage worked out the keys I would sing my songs in, and that night I sang. I wasn't particularly noticed. The majority of the audience were jiving to the music, some listened and seemed to like me but they didn't go mad. But the musicians noticed because later on in their 'office' — the pub round the corner — they said, 'Well, we'd like to hire you and we'll give you six pounds a week.' I said, 'Make it seven,' and they said, 'OK.' That was probably the first and last time in my life that I had any business acumen. I should have said ten. Anyway, I was hired to sing with John Dankworth.

From then on it was John Dankworth and the Johnny Dankworth Seven who influenced me. I learned all about music and musical taste. I often wondered why this band, the *crème de la crème* of musicians in those days, chose me as a singer and yet other bands didn't. Then I heard John tell somebody asking the same question, 'Well, all the other girls I interviewed and listened to — and there were a lot — all sounded like the current singer of the day. Cleo didn't, and that's what I was looking for — someone different.'

He was right. Most of the bands were looking for a substitute Doris Day, Teresa Brewer, Kay Star. Even though I sang the popular commercial songs, I never, ever wanted to sing like anybody else. I never wanted to sing the same routine, I always wanted to change it to suit me. Even if they ad-libbed, I would work out a different ad-lib, so as to avoid doing the song in exactly the same way as other singers.

John is responsible for a great deal of my musical education and inspiration. When I joined the band I was musically illiterate. I had a very low contralto voice and a narrow range. It was very frustrating, sitting on the bandstand night after night listening to them playing marvellous jazz solos, improvisations, and not really being able to do it myself because I didn't have the technique or the range. I only had an octave and a bit, which is very small for any kind of singer. I realized if I was going to get on I would have to improve my vocal equipment, so that's what I did.

Over many months, John raised the keys of songs I had to sing and gradually I became capable of singing in a higher key; that's how I learned about modulation — singing in one key and changing to another within the song. Later on I learned how to read music, although not as well as I should! I did it all through John Dankworth and the Dankworth Seven.

John knows my voice so well now, when he writes a song he knows just what's going to fit and where. Sometimes he writes things that are very difficult and I say, 'It's impossible. I can't sing that!' He'll say, 'Go away and try, because I know that you can. You'll find a way.' He knows there's something there that I don't know at the time. Inevitably, I go away and I do find a way. He continually challenges my vocal ability and has done for a great deal of our relationship. On top of that, he knows I've done extremely difficult work that he hasn't written and I've done it by myself.

But my musical career could never have happened in the same way had I joined another band. Not by any stretch of the imagination. It's the result of a sheer chance meeting and my own desire and determination to constantly improve my voice.

Ella Fitzgerald is another inspiration. She's a darling lady, not only in terms of being an excellent and great singer, technically and sound-wise, but to me she's someone within the jazz world who's a great example. She's stood proud and classy, she's never had any drug problems or done anything to give jazz a bad name. She's always been a great flag-waver for jazz and made it respectable. Some might say that's awful, but in a way jazz has to have that kind of aura of respectability to be recognized as an art form.

I admire tremendously the singers and musicians who have, against all the odds, battled on and done their work without degrading themselves or the music. Sadly, most people only admire those who've died under horrible conditions. They forget the ones who are alive and who've kept their noses clean and are still playing and singing good jazz.

I know some audiences go for the drama, the unpredictability of the artist, before the musical content. I've never understood that, or audiences that like to be insulted by an artist. There are lots of singers who go on the stage and verbally abuse an audience, as well as singing badly, and audiences seem to like it. I would never go and see anyone who did that to me. If anyone kept me waiting for an hour before I got to see them on stage, I'd never go again. I think it's very unprofessional. If you go to the theatre or a concert and it starts at eight o'clock, there should be no more than five or ten minutes' delay, not because of the artist, but because the audience is late getting seated.

Have you set yourself goals?

Nowadays, a lot of young people set themselves a time limit and if they've not made it in show business within that time-scale, they give up and plump for security. I think you should keep going. Things change, you turn corners unexpectedly. You must keep yourself open for the challenges that do come along. Like my first acting job.

I had never acted before but I had decided, even after everything they had given me, singing with the band was not going to get me any further. I would sit on the bandstand for the rest of my life and that would be it. So I decided I had to leave the band and look for something different. I told John I was leaving and he asked me to marry him! Again, I suspected he just wanted a cheap singer! I accepted his proposal and left anyway. It was 1958, and I'd been asked to audition for a play at the Royal Court Theatre. Even though I suspected it would probably only be a 'who's for tennis?' walk-on part, I was nevertheless happy to go along.

They knew nothing about me. They gave me the part to read, I learned it and read it, they discovered I could sing a bit as well, and I sang them a song. Eventually I was offered and accepted the lead in *Flesh to a Tiger*, a West Indian play by Barry Reckord. It was a great success and that was the start of my acting career. I thought, 'That's it — the change I wanted. I've become an actress; that's my life settled.' I was very disappointed I had to wait two years before I was offered another part, and just to keep my hand in, I went on tour with a play that wasn't very good.

Eventually I had to go back to singing, but not with the John Dankworth band. For a long while I did solo cabaret work and any acting jobs came along from time to time. Gradually the acting offers gathered momentum and, although it's very hard to accomplish when you start out as a singer, I began to be thought of as an actress as well.

George Devine at the Royal Court was someone who helped me a great deal. He said I had great potential and a natural instinct for acting and I shouldn't give up, I should keep going. I wasn't just a one-off play person, I had talent. He was very encouraging and that allowed me to go on and do other things.

Later, Frank Dunlop, now the Edinburgh Festival director, had a lot of faith in me as an actress, and in 1968 I played Lysistrata in *The Trojan Women*; then Hyppolita and Titania in *Midsummer Night's Dream*; the maid in *The Lesson*; *Hedda Gabler*; and Julie in the big smash hit West End production of *Showboat*.

I've a wide variety of acting experience. I can play tragic and dramatic roles, and over the years a comic streak has crept in which is developing nicely, so as I get older I'll be able to play funny old ladies!

Tell me how you deal with criticism, both professional, and from family and friends.

Professional criticism is part of show business. When it comes to critical music reviews, *I* know when I'm singing good, and *I* know when I'm off, and whether the programme content is good or bad.

I find reviewers are not very objective, they are very personal. They either like you or they don't. If you sing songs they don't like they won't say, 'Well, I didn't like it, but I thought she sang it well.' They are always either out-and-out jazz buffs and dislike the mixed programmes, or they're pure pop fanatics who don't like jazz programmes. So you really can't win. I know some reviewers who adore me and will give me a good review even when I don't deserve it. But that doesn't please me either.

I go out there and sing only for the audience that pays to come and hear me. It's important that *they* like me and continue to come along, to listen and enjoy my work. I'm well aware critics can effectively dissuade an audience from coming to a show. They can cause trouble for theatrical productions, but that doesn't happen with concerts. You have your fans and they come whether the critics like you or not.

My last dramatic role was on Broadway in *The Mystery of Edwin Drood*. It was a great success and I was nominated for Best Actress in a Broadway musical. I'm glad I decided for some reason — perhaps I'd just had enough — not to do it in London, because it wasn't well received by the critics. It would have been very sad to play the same role here and find the reviewers didn't like it. That would really have hurt.

John and I seldom get bad reviews for our concerts in America. It's not always so in Britain. But then again, here, any visiting fireman is given a better review than someone homegrown.

Living and working closely with John must make giving and taking criticism difficult. How do you manage it?

In recording sessions, John might say something doesn't fit and

I'll say, 'But I like doing it that way.' Then I'll think about it, try it his way and if I think it works better I'll keep it in. Out of respect to the composer I often have to do what he wants up to a point. After all, he wrote it and you don't change Beethoven, so why should I change John Dankworth! Occasionally I'll fight if there's something I feel very strongly about and, depending on how strongly John feels about it, the one who can persuade the other of the right way to go wins.

We do have fights sometimes, verbal punch-ups, but in the end it's the music that wins out, simply because if you argue about something that could eventually turn out awful, and John feels so very strongly my way is wrong, I'm not going to say, 'Up you: I'm doing it my way anyway!' And vice versa. If I feel strongly it's not right for me, that it won't work that way, then he'll relent. But that's only in the music. Otherwise it's like all marriages, we compromise a lot and work things through together. We have our battles; we're not all lovey-dovey and light; it's impossible after being married for thirty years, we couldn't have kept it up. Marriage is about compromise and it comes into our music as well.

How do you relax?

Walking. John and I have a house in California, in the wine district 40 miles north of San Francisco. It's the most beautiful countryside, the state parks, the sea. We go there and walk in Muir Woods among the great big redwood trees, which are absolutely magnificent.

Sitting. You think you are doing nothing but it's re-charging.

Looking into space. Especially John. You see him sitting looking out at the hills. He also enjoys do-it-yourself.

I read and embroider. You can think at the same time as embroidering. When I was in *Edwin Drood* I embroidered two chairs.

I hate holidays lazing about on beaches. We had a house in Malta when the children were young, so we visited the beach a lot. I enjoyed playing games with them but I hate sunbathing.

Have you had to make any sacrifices?

Work took me away from my children a lot when they were growing up. But it wasn't really a sacrifice. I don't think I could have said, 'Right, I'm going to stop everything and look after you.'

I wouldn't have been happy and I think they would have suffered, really suffered, because I would have hated it and been a miserable, rotten mother. Eventually I think they realized that, although not when they were younger. That pounding on the lavatory door, crying, 'Mummeeeeee!' That was when I really wanted a job to go to. I felt trapped. I was happier when they got older and understood why I had to go off and work.

Have you ever had to face failure?

When I wasn't taken up at auditions. I endured rejection for a long time. But I thought, 'Bugger them! I'll get there in the end anyway.'

I suppose *Colette* was my worst failure. John wrote both the book and the music, but it was my idea. I researched Colette for a long, long time and tried to get a lot of people to write it before John. For some reason or other people couldn't, or wouldn't — whatever. I always felt that Colette was right for me and I had this burning desire to play her. We had a lot in common: a black relative — her grandfather, her love for her mother, and her mother as an influence. We also shared a love of words, for me not so much as a writer but as a singer and actress. Aspects of her philosophy of life appealed to me as well.

John's music was marvellous. Eventually people will realize it was good regardless of the reviews it received. I didn't read all of them, but I knew they weren't good and it hurt because Colette was my baby. But I'm a pick-yourself-up, dust-yourself-off person and that wasn't going to destroy me. If I'd taken it to heart I would have given up.

I think my determination to carry on goes back to my mother. She was very much like that. She had a really hard, hard time but she kept going, struggling to rise up and out of the life she led, running boarding houses, cafés, hotels, etc. My father wasn't always easy to get along with; he had a chip on his shoulder and thought people didn't like him because of his colour. I'm sure he must have had some hard knocks during the thirties, when he couldn't get work, but she took the full brunt of his anguish and sensitivity, and just kept trundling on.

My mother gave me the sense of myself that says, 'No one is going to grind me down.' I know what I can and can't do and whether I'm doing it right or not. It makes me laugh when I read someone being described as too perfect — it's impossible to go on stage and be *perfect*, it can't happen. You can be singing a song and suddenly something goes wrong. You think, 'Why did that happen? It's destroyed what's gone before.' There's always something slightly off. The moments of perfection are rare indeed. Every artist strives to achieve it, but few reach the perfection they strive for.

I'm very self-critical. I hate listening to my own records because I know I could go back and do it again, even better. I love performing because I don't have to listen to myself. I hate concerts being recorded; I know they're very popular but I hate it just the same. I believe it's your persona, the image, that's as important as the music. If something goes wrong, you cover up with your personality, that's the art of peforming. Perhaps I hate listening to my own recordings because I haven't quite accomplished the art of covering up while recording!

When do you feel most vulnerable?

That's a hard question. The word vulnerable is so difficult, what does it mean? You don't know until something happens to crush you, then you're open to many painful moments.

For me it's big parties, I hate them. I have to go to them quite often and I have to psych and pump myself up to become the actress. I hate the superficiality — walking into a room with lots of strangers and having to think of something intelligent to say; people have such high expectations of you — *the special singer*, when you're really no different from anyone else. I don't like dos where you stand about making smalltalk while balancing food and drink that never seems to get to your mouth! But over the years I've discovered, if you dig deep enough and ask the right questions straight out, you can usually find someone interesting to talk to or learn from. Men always like talking about themselves; women are more reticent.

After a concert I'll always linger and take a deep breath before braving the crowds. What do you say to people who say, 'I thought that was marvellous!' or 'I think you are wonderful'? All you can say is, 'Thank you, thank you, thank you.' What else can you say?

That part of my work is hard, but at the same time, if it wasn't there, that would be awful, too. I know in a way they are reinforcing the skills I know I possess. I think I would feel most vulnerable if I did my concerts all over the world and no one came backstage afterwards. I'd wonder why and what had happened.

It doesn't worry me so much in the theatre. After the first weeks of a successful show, people don't come round every night and say, 'Well done.' The congratulations become more intermittent.

Do you get angry?

Yes, and I have to get rid of it very quickly. If I don't it seethes to a point where it becomes quite vicious and frightening. I shake, go hot and then I really let fly. So I have to get rid of my anger or whatever upsets me before it reaches boiling point. I'm a fishwife and a thrower. I saw my mother and father fight like cat and dog and even though it was frightening to us as kids, I always felt that expressing anger was much healthier than two people living together, silently resenting each other. It's very important to say what you don't like, and get it out.

Of what are you most proud?

Certainly I'm proud of my musical achievements, but especially a couple of records, the poetry albums, 'Shakespeare and all that jazz', and 'Wordsongs'. I feel those two are me; they were written especially for me and my voice. And another record called 'One more day'. I think that one is special because it was my baby. I thought of the idea and chose the writer and musicians.

I'm very proud of *Colette* and how that came about, and the work we all put into it.

I'm proud of my marriage and my children. They are all good, great kids. There's Stuart from my first marriage. He's a graphic designer, married and lives in California. He teaches soccer and runs soccer camps. American kids love it. It's not as highly competitive as it is here but I think eventually they will get a world team together, because the youngsters are beginning to take it seriously, although not as seriously as baseball and American football.

Stuart and I have a running joke between us. I say I've disowned him as my son in public because he's too old for me now. He's my brother, or nephew!

Alec is an excellent bass player, at present on tour in Asia with the Clark Tracey Band. It's his daughter I'm babysitting.

My daughter Jacqueline went to the Guildhall School of Music and Drama and is an actress and a very good singer. I told her the crossover from actress to singer is easier than singer to actress, so get yourself established as an actress first. And, would you believe it, she took Mum's advice!

Do you have a personal vision?

It would be lovely if there was more peace in the world. It doesn't feel peaceful at the moment, it's so unsettled and scary; wars, fighting — Iran, Ireland, Israel. I think war is an abomination!

I'm very happy and proud of doing what I'm doing now. I realize that as I get older the voice may go and I'll have to come to terms with that. How, I don't know exactly. But I hope I'll be clever enough to say so if I hear it going, and stop singing. I don't want to carry on unless it pleases me 90 per cent of the time. But, having heard so many that don't stop, I might be the same, but I hope I'm not.

In the main, it's been singing that's been my glory. When I'm on stage singing well it's joyful and I'm happy. That's where I come alive. I would be very unhappy if I didn't sing, although sometimes I wonder why I'm doing it. I say, 'I could be a bus conductress and be much happier!' But I know that's only a joke.

I'm never drained after a performance, often it's before. It's very odd because the story goes that at the age of three I was in a dancing class and we had to do a concert locally for the Southall working men's club. My sister was a dancer and was to dance while I sang a song, but because I was so anxious, I wouldn't go on and sing the song. Eventually, she pulled me on stage because she wanted to do her dance, and once there I sang my song over and over again and she had to then pull me off! And that's how it's been ever since. Getting me to sing is difficult but once I'm on, I love it. I've found it's easier to fight the fear of going on by taking deep breaths before getting up to sing.

Getting off gracefully was another problem for a while. Once, when I was on the same Sunday concert bill as two singers called the Tanner Sisters, they said to me, 'You walk on like an elephant, but when you get to the microphone you are marvellous, then you back off like a giraffe!' So I worked hard at it and I think I walk on quite regally most of the time now!

Linda Bellos.

Linda Bellos

Former Leader, Lambeth Council

I was very keen to meet Linda Bellos to see if she lived up to her Loony Left, tabloid press image. I found Linda to be a committed socialist, remarkably honest and an uncomfortably pragmatic and astute politician.

Who has inspired you over the years?

It sounds a bit twee, but when I was young I was inspired by the idea of Joan of Arc, not so much because of the religious questions that surrounded her — was she or wasn't she a heretic? — much more because she was a woman who had a point of view and was prepared to die for it. I felt that was inspirational. I'm not particularly enamoured of death, but I feel very strongly about sincerity of belief.

People of courage inspire me: Paul Robeson, and, in the 1960s and 1970s particularly, Angela Davis and Martin Luther King Jr. I'm inspired by strong women: Adrienne Rich, Audrey Lord. Later on my inspiration came not so much from individual heroines and heroes but through reading the detail of what happened to the Jews during the Holocaust and the Nazi occupation of Poland. The South African political situation is another example. Anywhere there are acts of heroism and a maintenance of clarity, dignity, faith and hope, in spite of overwhelming odds — all that I find inspiring. I've never read anyone's life history and aspired to be like them. It's being enriched by the knowledge of individuals who have withstood tremendous pressure and maintained their integrity, that's what I find inspiring.

Has that inspiration been the motivation for what you are doing now?

No. My life and work today are almost the result of a series of coincidences. I was born in 1950. As well as being black, I'm also Jewish, and one of the first very significant things in my life I can remember is my mother forcing me to watch the Eichmann trial.

For many children born around that time, the Second World War was very much in our psyche, even though we hadn't personally experienced it. In London, where I grew up, we were surrounded by the bomb sites and, as a very young child, I asked myself what *I* would have done in such a situation. I don't know if other people did the same. For me, being black meant there was an additional vulnerability from the threat of facism, but because I'm black, people don't recognize I'm Jewish as well. For various reasons, I had to ask the question, 'What would I have done in that situation, as a black person and as a Jew?' Racism plays a significant part in who I am and what motivates me.

I remember, aged six or seven, being in the classroom and saying nothing when another black child was being humiliated. It only happened once, but that once was enough for me. I felt ashamed for not having spoken up and I vowed I would never allow a situation to arise where injustice was done in my presence and I said nothing. Children know what injustice is. They know right from wrong. I learned it was wrong to get off the bus without paying your fare. I'm not saying I'm perfect; I do wrong things sometimes, but I *know* they're wrong and I don't pretend they're right. So I've always intervened against that kind of treatment. Wherever I am, perhaps on the street, seeing an old lady being hassled, I'll say something, whatever the consequences. I started on the road to where I am now, fighting injustice, that long ago.

I moved away from London and got married, had my children and was political in that I joined the Labour Party. I first became actively involved in community politics when I campaigned to save the local nursery from closure. My husband was unemployed when my second child was born, so I went back to work. I was breast-feeding and working full-time. It was very painful and tiring.

I had several different jobs; manual work, which to varying degrees, was unpleasant; I worked in kitchens and factories, and finally got a job with the Inland Revenue which was, relatively, more pleasant. This was three months after the birth of my second

Paul Robeson. Reproduced courtesy of Popperfoto.

child. I was exhausted; I had two children, I breast-fed, I didn't drive, I struggled on and off buses with them and did a hard day's work, came home and cooked the tea. I knew it would continue like that unless I did something about it. I was 25 or 26. Then, one morning during a six o'clock feed, I looked into my daughter's eyes and I thought to myself, 'Where will I be in ten years' time?' I said to her in my head, 'I've got to do something with my life. I can't carry on like this.'

I decided to resign from my job, go to university, take my driving test and have an abortion, because I discovered I was pregnant again. It was being pregnant again, being so tired. I had a two-year-old and a three-month-old baby. I know I couldn't have gone through with the third pregnancy. It would have been the end of me. I owed it to my children to not be frustrated and live my life through them, or sacrifice my life to them and then be resentful. I owed it to myself and to them to do something, and I did. I didn't discuss it with my husband. I got up, went to work and rang him from work, and said, 'I'm going to resign.' I gave a month's notice.

Did you have support for that decision?

Yes. From my friends. One of them had gone to university and another was considering it. I also had friends, university lecturers, who gave me a great deal of encouragement.

I applied for my driving test, applied to university as a mature, unqualified student, and chose Sussex because it was just up the road and I had to be near my family. My next door neighbour, with three children, went there. I thought, 'She's done it and so can I,' so I grasped the nettle, studied politics and read Marx.

I arranged my tutorials around my children, who were at school and playschool. It sounds difficult, but compared to full-time work it was a cinch. I did have to get up at five in the morning and write essays, before my children got up, or work until three the night before, but I survived. In the process of studying, the scales fell from my eyes. I became a feminist.

What is your definition of a feminist?

Oh dear! I don't particularly have a clear definition of a feminist in so far as there are lots of women who read *Spare Rib* and regard themselves as feminists. I think a feminist actively participates in attempting to end the oppression of women. That must be the relevant criterion and that leaves a broad enough definition to allow it to be manifested in a number of ways. Lots of women can call themselves feminists. They don't have to be all in the same campaigns, doing the same things in the same way. We are all seeking to change society in our different ways and I think that's fine. After all, the oppression of women manifests itself in different ways, so why not have the 300 Group pushing for 50 per cent female MPs? I'm not going to join, but it doesn't stop me doing what I want to do, and neither am I going to stop that group from doing things the way they want to.

What happened after university?

In 1981, I ceased being married and moved back to South London. I got involved in a group called Women Against Violence Against Women and took a job on *Spare Rib* magazine as journalist and finance worker. It was a wonderful period, deeply and actively political. It was traumatic in lots of ways as well, but it was exciting; it was real politics; we were a small group of women and we put violence against women on the public agenda. At the time we couldn't have anticipated the result of our campaigning, but I feel we are now reaping the benefit of our effects and actions.

Mary Whitehouse was very much in evidence then. We raised the feminist analysis of pornography. We pointed the finger at men, rape, prostitution, incest. We linked up with Rape Crisis centres, Women's Aid and Lesbian Line. We raised uncomfortable issues and brought them to the fore. We allowed women to talk about things they hadn't had the opportunity to talk about before, even though they were worried, frightened and in some cases traumatized by them. We wrote newspaper and magazine articles, spoke to the Women's Institutes, Housewive's Register, schools. We were out and about lobbying, organizing street demos. I was as busy then as I am now.

Gradually the pressure on the group mounted. We became exhausted. We were being attacked from all sides, politically. I got very frustrated with the women's liberation movement. I found it white and racist. They were exploring their racism but in a very self-indulgent way — breast-beating. It was all guilt and no action.

I left *Spare Rib*, took a job as community accountant in Lambeth, about 100 yards from the Town Hall. I had learned a lot about organization and bureaucracy working in the Civil Service; how it worked and how necessary bureaucracy is. But I had the desire to temper it. I wanted to share out the power of bureaucracy. Most people have no power over bureaucracy because they don't know how it operates. It's something monolithic that strikes them down. People say negative things about bureaucracy. I don't think there is anything intrinsically wrong with it — it's the negative way it's used. I then took a job in the GLC Women's Unit and during that period I was invited to become a councillor on Lambeth borough council.

How did you feel about that invitation?

In a funny way, I was a little resentful. I had just applied for a job within Lambeth Council but I had to withdraw my application to become a councillor.

For many of us the GLC was a key. It demonstrated openly and practically how bureaucracy can be used positively. Under close scrutiny some of the more bizarre things that were claimed to be happening at the time didn't happen at all. The GLC achieved a great deal in terms of raising public awareness. Ken Livingstone's adminstration proved that things *could* be changed and that had a tremendous impact on working-class people, not just for those living in London, but outside as well. It proved there was a point in intervention and a point in using the political process. A healthy democracy must instill into society some enthusiasm for the political process, the act of participation, whether you simply use your vote or become an active political representative.

There's some logic in my choosing to enter community politics. I'm not unique; there are many of us throughout London and the rest of the country who've chosen to actively participate in the Labour Party by becoming councillors. We believe we can make a valuable contribution despite working under a Tory government for so long. To a tremendous extent, Tory central government restricts the ability of a group of councillors to carry out socialist policies. Nevertheless, we can still change things.

I want to see a radical transformation of society. I want to see the end of capitalism, but I don't think it comes about by staying ideologically pure, or being an armchair socialist with grand theories, talking in wonderful Marxist language to other people who understand what you're talking about. That won't move 'the Revolution' forward.

Angela Davis. Reproduced courtesy of Popperfoto.

I believe equality and justice can be delivered. We may not
be able to do it to the extent that we would like, but that is active
socialism. The GLC showed it works. They raised controversial
issues and something positive came out at the end.

What's the alternative to capitalism?

I haven't got a blueprint. Whose blueprint would it be? A male
blueprint? If so, how do the rest of us participate in that process?
What happens to our vision of how it should be? I have a vision
of a society that is free of exploitation and injustice, and I don't
think we'll take a magical leap and get there. I think we have to
work at it, at how we relate to each other now, how we deliver
power and share that power — now. That's part of the changing
process. We have to be flexible; someone else's idea might be as
good as mine. They all have to be considered.

That can be frightening for people who may not share your vision. Most people appear to want the security of a blueprint that doesn't exist.

I don't agree with you. Look what's been happening for the last
eight years. Have people had a vision? No. Not of any kind, not
even one that I can disagree with. I'm talking about the majority
of people, the 46 per cent or so who vote Tory. They've not got
a vision, the comfort of knowing where Toryism is leading them,
because the Tories have never made clear at the outset where
they plan to lead people. People who might have been deemed
to be Tory supporters have become unemployed; their trade union
rights have been eroded. This is what the Tories have done to
their own supporters.

I regret the Labour Party has not put forward a viable alternative
vision, and in that context people have voted for the devil they
know. It's not fair of you to ask me what vision I would put in
its place. I'm not the leader of the Labour Party, but I have no
illusions about the fact that the people are the future.

Is being a woman in intrinsic part of what you are doing? What do you bring to your job as a woman?

Yes. My feminist understanding is predicated on me being a
woman and seeing the world through the eyes of a woman in

a society that is dominated by men. I am conscious that the world is not neutral. We don't have a fair distribution of power or resources. Having said that, there are some contradictions for me. I was the leader of a council. It's not a feminist organization; it's a traditional organization and, in order to succeed in my vision of what I can do on a day-to-day basis, I have to act in a way that will be effective, the way men will understand. I suppose in a sense that compromises me. I don't feel that it does, but it probably does. I'm not compromising my principles, but how I achieve my goals.

What kind of support have you valued most?

The support of my friends, the overwhelming majority of whom are women. More specifically, black lesbians, friends who stuck by me during the difficult times as Council Leader. I'm not alone or unique within this Council; there are lots of us subject to similar pressures and recently, when I had a freak-out in a Council session, we decided to try to share the pressures we felt in order to avoid things getting on top of us. It's difficult enough finding the time to discuss such areas of responsibility and what we are trying to do, but we do try to provide each other with support and that's very important. Equally, the support I get from the black community, both in Brixton and Lambeth as a whole, as well as outside, is vital to me.

It's very easy when you're in a position of power to lose your mates and sense of purpose. You can be seduced by that power, but if you have close links with a community it's very hard to get away with being seduced; friends and political opponents won't let you get away with it. So I've consciously sought to maintain my links with the community.

How does this support manifest itself?

Not in an organized way. But, for example, a member of a black organization stopped me on my way in to the offices the other day and said, 'I understand you're getting a lot of pressure. We've talked about it within the community. How can we help?' I find that expression of concern very, very comforting, especially in the face of bitter internal arguments. It's very easy to get lost in arguments that most of the community, black and white, don't give a damn about! It's comforting and gratifying to have people

come up to you in the street and say, 'Keep up the good work.'
That's happened a lot over the past three months. It shows me
there's life outside that particular debate.

Do you have difficulty putting yourself first?

I try to look after myself. When the phone rings at home and
it's council business and I'm trying to have a night off I'll say, 'This
is my night off. Phone my office tomorrow.'

How do you have fun?

Dinner at home with friends.
   I've always been busy and involved. I've never had a
tremendous social life; I tend not to put that first. I ought to, but
politics comes first, whatever it might be — Labour Party debates
or campaigning for black sections. Politics have been my life for
a long time. I don't feel I'm sacrificing anything.
   Councillors are not paid, they receive a small daily attendance
allowance. I don't have any additional income and that's difficult.
I would like to have a weekend away but that costs money and
I can't do it. I'd like to go to the theatre more and to concerts.
I say that, but even when I do have the time and money I often
can't be bothered. Instead, I tend to enjoy myself and relax at
home with good food, something decent to drink and good
company.

Do you find it difficult to keep your
public and private lives separate?

I stopped eating out when I moved recently and got a decent
kitchen — it's less hassle. The good restaurants round here have
been taken over by yuppies, and hearing their loud, ignorant,
obnoxious conversations makes me angry. Last time I ate out,
a group of them were complaining loudly about the rates in the
borough, their dislike of arranged marriages, and other racist
nonsense. So as I left I remarked, 'The next time you complain
publicly about the rates, you'd do well to ensure the Leader of
the Council is not sitting at the next table!' In order to avoid that
kind of hassle it's better not to eat out, or else choose places where
I have a rapport with the usually black or Third World staff.
   I've almost completely stopped going to feminist events as well,

because I know ten minutes after arriving I'm going to be hassled, mainly on squatting, by white, downwardly mobile women who don't approve of the fact that Lambeth prefers to house working-class families with children in Council property. I fully support our housing policies and, much as I wish we were in a position to house all single people, we don't have enough homes. In my opinion, squatting is about the fit, queue-jumping at the expense of those who don't know how to do it and can't do it. I don't need to listen to this on my night off, when I'm trying to have a bit of fun, so I leave.

How do you deal with criticism?

It depends on the nature of the criticism. Some things I fully accept, like our inability to house everybody who needs to be housed. Often there is nothing we can do about some issues. Councillors are supposed to have the power to remedy deficiencies in the system, but very often we can't do so. That puts us in the front line for criticism. In that case, I will try and explain as clearly as I can exactly why we are unable to carry out our statutory obligations to the community.

On the whole, when I'm criticized I'll think it through, judge whether it's valid or not and try to remedy the situation. For example, my workload is very heavy; consequently there are communication difficulties. Colleagues may not be clear about what has been done and what needs to be done. We all frequently make a special effort to improve internal communications, but, due to the nature and stresses of the job, we get dragged back into our work in a way that makes it impossible.

What does success mean to you?

Obtaining a set of consistent monthly figures to monitor and circulate to the various Council officers, and for myself. We owed housing benefit to lots of working-class people living in the borough. We were not coping well with administering housing benefit after the hand-over from the DHSS, but we made significant progress in turning that situation round.

How about a personal achievement?

I'm too busy to think about such things and I don't think I would want to think about them anyway.

Have you had to make sacrifices and how do you feel about making them?

I feel privileged to be in a position to get some of my ideas implemented. Few people in this society have that opportunity. However, in financial terms the cost of having that power is considerable. As I said before, as a full-time Councillor I receive an attendance allowance of £16.70 a day, shortly to be increased to £17.55. With the additional subsistence sum, I end up, on a good month, with a cheque for about £520. While this may be more than some people earn, especially black women, I do resent the pay given, especially when it's compared to the Council staff wages, working less hours and with far less responsibilities.

Have you had to face failure? How did you cope?

Yes. Many times. Failing the 11-plus, because my failure was rubbed in unnecessarily. I try to learn lessons from my failures and re-think how to avoid making the same mistakes in the future.

What would you say have been your highest and lowest public and private moments?

My highest moment, publicly, was at a Lambeth black workers' conference where I got a standing ovation for a speech I made about the shortcomings of the Council and how they could be remedied.

My highest private moments are always dinner parties with my friends.

My lowest public moments are Labour group arguments and internal wrangling.

Privately, I hate having builders botch up repairs on my house.

When do you feel most vulnerable, professionally and personally?

Being in a Labour group; on my own makes me feel vulnerable, and, because I've been stopped so often by the police, asking where I'm going and what I'm doing, I feel vulnerable with a few black people in white areas. I feel when I'm in those areas I must take some form of personal identification with me.

How do you manage and control your anger?

Verbally. I shout and speak up against things.

What lessons have you learned in your life?

That if change was simple it would have happened years ago, therefore I must expect plenty of opposition and resistance to my ideas and proposals for that change.

Martin Luther King Jr. leading a protest march to the courthouse in Montgomery, Alabama, March 1965. Reproduced courtesy of Popperfoto.

Carole Tongue.

Carole Tongue

Member of the European Parliament

Carole's vivacity and refreshingly down to earth effectiveness as a politician impressed me enormously when I met her for the first time chairing a meeting on the EEC. In July 1984, aged 29, she was elected to the European Parliament. At that time she was the youngest British MEP. Commuting between Barking, where she lives, her consistuency, Strasbourg and Brussels, her feet seldom touch the ground. Her integrity and opinions are highly valued. She plied us with tea and biscuits and while listening and replying to our questions, she skilfully registered the 'multitude of messages stacking up on her answering machine.

In some ways I followed a non-traditional pattern for doing what I'm doing now. I left school with 11 O levels and some A levels, all languages. I then set about looking for a university course that was more practical than theoretical and combined languages with politics. Most language courses lead to teaching, business or international marketing and not much else. I was far more interested in politics, current affairs, and European affairs in general. I ended up at Loughborough University studying a new course then: languages, politics and economics of modern Europe. It was orientated towards working in the European community, and international organizations.

My own family is very international. I have five sisters. We are aged between 22 and 37 years and are from three different marriages and five nationalities. That's given me a different perspective, which is far from being chauvinistic. One sister is a lawyer, one an adviser on violence against women and in child abuse at the National Police Training College; one sister is at the

Institute of Linguists; one is a potter, another a psychologist. Three are in Switzerland and three in Britain.

My father is head of an international organization based in Switzerland. My mother is a physiotherapist and lives in England. She has been a member of the Labour Party since 1960 and my stepfather was in the Independent Labour Party in Scotland and has been in labour politics since the early '20s, and was a probation officer in the east end of London for 30 years after World War II.

It was his political experience and the experience of the living conditions that he saw in his job that had a profound effect on me, coupled with hearing knee-high to a sparrow, my mother's own life and work experience as a part-time worker in the health service: her working conditions; the low pay of part-time workers in a predominantly female profession, the low status; the struggles she faced when opting to join COHSE (a union which was traditionally for auxiliary workers), as opposed to remaining within her professional organization; how she was treated having Labour Party and CND stickers on her car, her struggle in the beginning as a one-parent family, and just generally not getting the respect and credit for what she did. Their experience contributed greatly to my early political education and was a spur to my later involvement in politics.

After six months at Loughborough, I thought, 'This is crazy! Jill of all trades, mistress of none, trying to do French, German, politics and economics, never having done economics before.' It was all too much. I asked if I could do three of the four options, but they said no, it's two of the four or it's the lot. So I switched to politics and French. It annoyed me to learn later they subsequently allowed students to do three of the four.

I finished the course with little or no direction; it was almost as if lecturers, thought, 'Oh well, Carole will just go through the academic field'. It was presumed I would somehow know what I would do — but I didn't. I regret I wasn't encouraged to go and do an MA and I wasn't given much advice by careers teachers at Loughborough.

After university I drifted into full-time employment as an assistant editor on a medical journal. That gave me good experience of editing, working in an office environment and I taught myself to type.

After a year I thought, what do I do now? I put in an application to the Civil Service to work as a news editor; got the job and turned it down because suddenly I thought, 'God, the Civil

Service! I can't go into this; I want to travel, build up my foreign languages'.

I took a job as a courier for a tour operator. I bundled off to the South of France for five months looking after British and Dutch tourists in mobile homes, gaining fluency in child care and plumbing French, learning how to get on with people. I returned home still fairly directionless, and went into secretarial temping for British Gas, and then thought I would do another season in France. This time I went to the west coast.

I made friends with a family who lived on the France/Luxembourg borders. Living in a French steel town and commuting daily into another country gave me an understanding of life in a heavy industrial town, of its people and of the life of frontier workers — all of which I draw on today in my work. I took temping jobs with the idea of getting into the administrative side of the European Parliament based in Luxembourg.

Unfortunately I just missed the entrance exam which only happens once every five years. But just as I was leaving, very dispirited, someone said, 'Ah, but you might be interested in the scholarship'. I pricked up my ears, and said, 'What's that?'

It was then I learned about the Robert Schuman Scholarship offering postgraduates work in the European Parliament for three months, researching, answering parliamentarians' questions. I got the last British vacancy for 1979 and did a Youth Unemployment Project — researching into how the European community had responded to the growth in young unemployed people.

That brought me back into the academic field, and I thought I would like to stay. Because there were so few graduate posts on offer, I accepted a secretarial post, which perhaps was unwise. Normally as a graduate you are not allowed to work in the European Parliament at secretarial level, but, as the post was in the Socialist Group, I thought, better to be in the political environment I wanted than wait around for a higher level posting.

In fact I was lucky, I ended up working for the deputy head of the Socialist Group administration department which had 70 people. He recognized my capabilities, gave me a lot of leeway in the work I did, and encouraged me to get involved in a wide range of issues. I got to know the subjects we followed quite well and I used the opportunity to make contacts, talk to MPs, do that unrequired extra bit of work. I did that for about four years.

Increasingly I became very frustrated with the absolutist approach of the Labour Party towards membership of the EEC;

plus I became aware of the half-truths being told. I wanted somehow to contribute to the Euro-election campaign. I thought I could perhaps go back to the UK and compile ammunition for candidates to use.

I was discussing this with three journalists, from the *Financial Times, Telegraph,* and *Guardian* in the bar in about June 1983 and the three of them chorused, 'Be a candidate'. I was amazed. These were three men, well known, and well respected in their field. I went away and had a think; my boss put himself in to be a candidate. I said what do you think about *my* standing? He said, 'Why not. Go for it! You know a lot more than others attempting to be a candidate.'

Fortunately, I had retained membership of Upminster Labour Party, where I had spent most of my life, and I wrote off to a number of wards, never thinking I would get beyond the first stages, let alone be selected, or elected.

I embarked on this project with more than a little trepidation, because I knew I would be up against people who had been in and around party politics in the labour movement for some time. I was right; it was a very hard fought seat. It was in Tory hands at the time but potentially winnable.

I had never spoken in public before other than to small groups, for example, Quaker school children visiting Brussels. With sweaty palms and knocking knees, I went to the first ward in Hornchurch and was chosen to speak to their general management committee but did not win their nomination.

Having grown up in Upminster, my parents and I were well known in the local Labour Party, and my local ward nominated me without seeing me. At the Upminster selection meeting I was against three men and I was terrified. I decided not to speak about myself at all. Other prospective candidates spoke about their long history of working in the trade unions, or Labour Party, etc. I chose not to do that. I felt very uncomfortable about selling myself in that way. I concentrated on what I felt the party needed to do at a European level and presented information they hadn't heard before, in a way that was new, blunt and honest.

I spoke about the EEC environment and equal opportunity policies, and social legislation — inadequate as it is. I said people had been told a series of half truths and sometimes even less than that. I also said we had been sold a negative stance which in part stemmed from a nationalistic and chauvinistic streak in the Labour Party which I very much wanted to combat.

It worked! I got 23 votes and the men got four votes between them! I couldn't believe it. I barely knew how to respond, let alone give an acceptance speech. I just said weakly, 'Thank you very much, I hope I'll go on and make a good candidate.'

I got pipped at the post in another constituency. I was up against a former Dagenham Labour MP, a male-dominated general committee, and a lot of male trade unionists. Yet this man only beat me by three votes, and that gave me a clue that people welcomed someone with a new approach.

I ended up with only *one* nomination from a total of nine constituencies and was up against the deputy international secretary of the Labour Party who had *five* nominations. I went in convinced he had already won.

I overheard his speech and again he sold himself on his greater experience in the Labour movement. Once more I stuck to stating what I thought needed to be done, by the Labour movement at European level and concentrated on outlining policies I thought would be interesting and which probably hadn't been aired in public before.

I won 54 votes to 48. I was completely overwhelmed; you could have knocked me down with a feather.

I find this difficult to say, but it came back to me on the grapevine that people found my speech very moving. I think I do speak from my heart and gut. I felt so passionately about equal opportunities, and was frustrated and angry with the Neanderthal approach of the Labour movement, particularly the trade union movement towards the EEC who often chose to ignore the EEC's equal opportunities policies. This, thank goodness, is starting to change.

Perhaps there's a message there. If you think you are not going to get something, you may go in more honest, more forthcoming because you've nothing to lose. My message to women is, don't be put off by the competition you think may exist. Don't do yourself down at all. So what if you don't get selected or even elected first time. It's all good experience.

What is the source of your passions?

My passion arises from a sense of indignation about the way the vast majority of women are forced to lead their lives; the limited expectations of what they are capable of achieving; the doors never opened to them; the constraints upon their lives; all of

which I have learned more and more about through the women
I know.

My heroines are less Sylvia and Cristobel Pankhurst, and Dora
Russell, who are certainly heroines, but more the women Ford
machinists, the Barking hospital domestic cleaners, and the raw
deal they got. They are really the inspiration that drives me on.

The Ford women grapple daily with three different groups of
men, in a male dominated environment; the employers, trade
unionists and their partners. They came out on strike — I gave
what assistance and support I could. Along with Jo Richardson
MP, I used my position to threaten the employers and sometimes
the trade unions. It was great to be able to give some support
and fight together with them. These women were heroines. They
were doing something they had never done before — taking
militant action; in the case of the Barking hospital women, sticking
it out on a picket line for a year.

During the Ford dispute I had a visit from a Head Office
manager, dying to impress me. He asked when could he show
me round the Dagenham plant and I replied, 'When the women
get equal pay for equal work' — and I meant it!

Is it their raw courage that inspires you?

Very much so. To take on the formidable patriarchy of the Ford
Motor Company or of trade unions . . . They were so isolated,
lacking in support for what they were trying to do. It's seeing
that hard struggle; seeing Tessa, who works with me, get up, do
the breakfast, prepare lunch for the children, work for me, then
go to pick up her kids from school, do the ironing, housework,
never having a moment to herself to breathe. It wasn't until
recently she felt confident enough to be able to answer, at the
age of 34, when her teenage son asked why she was going out,
'Because I *want* to, Anthony!'

I've learned that people are divided into different classes, in
terms of opportunity between the likes of me and Tessa, my
assistant, or Kathy, who works with us in the house. The dividing
factor is tertiary education: what it does for you, the doors it opens
for you. All that is expected of women without it, leaving school
at 16, is marriage, children and a job that is totally secondary in
their lives.

Recently I asked the father of a 14-year-old Newham girl taking
A levels what he thought his daughter was going to go on and

do. He said: 'I expect she'll become a PA to some important man'. I think that father's response accurately reflects the limited expectations of the vast majority of girls now. It's so important for girls to know there is a lot more to life, and with a little bit of space and encouragement they can be like Tessa, doing a degree at 34 through evening classes.

Women like Tessa and Kathy have taught me, not only how privileged I am, but that I've been in a position from the word go, to say: 'I want to go ahead and do X, Y, and Z.' I come from a middle class background, privileged in terms of education, though not money. We had books and stimulation in the house; my mother had done four years' professional training. It was taken for granted I would go on to higher education. There was support, and moving into a profession, a well-paid job, was something that was held up for me and the way was facilitated. 10 to 15 per cent of the population are similarly privileged. That leaves 85 per cent that are not. That makes me see how privileged I am and spurs me on to open more doors for women like Tessa.

What are your goals, personally and politically?

Firstly, to get the British Labour movement to think a bit more European; to think beyond national frontiers; to confront the fact we live in a multi-national economy and that increasingly the margin of manoeuvre for any government or trade union movement is restricted at a national level.

I want to bring Britain out of our present geographical and even spiritual isolation and invite people to look beyond British borders to other countries; to the continent; to show them Europeans are not green with pink horns and red spots. I want everyone I come in contact with to realize there is life beyond Dover!

A lot of my work over the last year has been with various trade unions, encouraging meetings with representatives of other unions in community countries. I think this has helped them realize that workers in all countries face common problems and that the high rate of unemployment, the introduction of new technology for example, is not peculiar to the UK. I want to highlight the need for extra-national policies and for the trade unions to develop a European agenda.

Secondly, to improve equal opportunities. If I could help get an EEC law of maternity rights and benefits implemented, then I would feel the work and occasional disappointments would have been worthwhile. Currently Britain has the worst level of maternity benefit of any western country, from Finland to Portugal.

At present (October 1987) we are faced with legislation that will disenfranchise 50 per cent of women workers from any kind of employment protection. Current government proposals mean that part-time workers (90 per cent of whom are women) would have to work for *five years* with the same company before being entitled to get antenatal and maternity leave, and the right to job reinstatement. Not only that but she would have to work 20 hours, not 16, to qualify for those rights and benefits, and full-time workers will have to work for *two years* with the same company before they can qualify for benefits.

Thirdly, I want to strengthen the hand of women in the trade union movement. I hope that by giving information, support, the pressure I and my colleagues can bring to bear on certain issues, and my own political experience will help women trade unionists. I want women to generate their own European agenda; to develop their demands for what they want an EEC equal opportunities unit to do. I believe things are beginning to crystalize; 1988 will see the first conference for European women trade unionists. It will bring together women who have been trying to put EEC law into practice at grassroots level.

I am a member of the EEC Committee on the Environment, Consumer Protection and Public Health, and am very concerned about the environment. Another political goal would be to see protection of the environment as an integral part of economic policy and not just part of the brown-rice-open-toed-sandal-brigade's woolly-minded, middle class do-gooding agenda. I want to raise people's awareness and communicate the fact it makes economic as well as human sense to preserve the environment. To draw attention to this and make my work relevant to the people I represent, I try to vulgarize issues, for example, by publicy throwing my aerosol cans into my dustbin in an attempt to encourage people to reduce their use and thus slow down the destruction of the earth's ozone layer.

Is your public and private life ever in conflict?

Yes, there is a conflict exacerbated by the fact I am single, and I am therefore expected to be able to do much more than married colleagues. We have been conditioned by male MPs to believe it is only work *outside* the home that is important; that roaring up and down the country speaking at meetings seven days and nights a week is quite acceptable and par for the course. Trying to break with that tradition is very difficult, coupled with which my experience of women parliamentarians is that we do twice as much as the men anyway, because not only are we trying to prove ourselves to be as good as they are, we take on the equal opportunities dossier, and, with all that it comprises, it automatically *doubles* your workload, especially if you want to make yourself accountable to the women you represent.

Political parties don't believe in the need for a private life, and I think until we get male allies saying: 'No, I'm not doing a meeting on a Sunday,' and setting limits, we will never see a change in these excessive and unreasonable personal demands.

Being in the public eye, and an MEP, doesn't encourage the appearance of soul mates, or a partner. Men seem easily deterred, no matter how approachable you are.

I feel trapped in a culture that is biased towards the traditional nuclear family and which discriminates against single people. I don't go to discotheques and clubs. I haven't time to socialize in that way and in my working environment and age group there are very few single men.

I haven't got a soul mate to come home to and pour out my troubles to. It is an incredibly lonely life. Coming home to an empty house isn't much fun after a while. I have fantastic female friends but if I were to do another term I would have to seriously consider combining households with a girlfriend, because I need the mutual support that would give. I don't recommend living alone and doing this job. While you do get emotional support, mainly from women colleagues and friends, you miss out on that crucial intimate support you get from a partner bathing away the sores of the day, and maybe helping you to see what you thought was a damn-awful meeting in an objective light. That kind of loneliness is really hard, and I don't always know how to overcome it. You might think I meet tons of people. I do. I also get approached by a lot of married men who would like an attractive, convenient mistress while in Strasbourg, but they get pretty short shrift! That's not what I'm interested in. It's hard without a soul mate and it's hard to find there's no other alternative but to pay other women to help you in the house.

As a feminist, asking other women to clean and help me presents a huge conflict. I think cleaning co-ops would change the difficult relationship between female cleaners and their employers. I hate the fact it's isolated women doing domestic work in other people's houses but I don't have any other option. I could not manage without domestic help of some kind. I know I share this experience with many women — single, separated or divorced. We all say the same thing: the men get their social life arranged for them by their wives; but how do we organize a dinner party? I'm giving my second one since 1984 next month. A girlfriend is helping me, but it's a tremendous strain.

If you can't socialize because of a hectic timetable, you're forgotten; people think you're not around. I do get invited out more now, but it's not at all easy. Most married male colleagues don't need to make the same kind of effort.

Traditionally men have compartmentalized their lives, never letting their personal lives encroach upon their professional lives; but I think being human is being political. Men have a lot to gain from being given the space to be themselves away from work.

I think the way you treat people is very important. I judge my colleagues on the basis of how I see them treat their staff or members of their family. I have often written someone off, no matter what they say on the platform, because they don't bear out what they say in their human relationships. I place a high premium on what someone is like as a person, and there's not enough of that in political life.

How do you cope with failure?

Sometimes I think I fail in my job because I find working in such a male-dominated sphere very intimidating. The macho behaviour of certain male colleagues flexing their political muscles is very alienating, very boring and, within your own party, often highly competitive. It's so bad at some meetings I fail to contribute at all, opt out and carry on as best I can from the outside. I feel I just do not want to get involved with it. I succeed by exerting pressure, influence from outside the male-dominated power base. But I would much rather work in co-operation and collaboration with colleagues. It doesn't happen often and that can be very depressing.

The current political climate (a third term of Tory government) is particularly disappointing and depressing. Keeping your optimism and enthusiasm going is very difficult. Inspiration comes from those worse off than you; support comes from colleagues and friends, and their appreciation and reliance on you encourages you to keep going.

My life tends to be full of enormous highs and massive lows. I think that is the destiny of many women in this society, where things don't always come right; you believe it's all worked out; you may have a satisfying job; you can achieve great things but not have great happiness at home.

I get a great high talking to young people at school who seem very interested in what I'm doing and want to learn more about it.

I was over the moon when the Ford women strikers won their case. It was 1984 and in total the dispute had been going on for 16 or more years.

How do you manage the low times?

If I'm sitting down on a Saturday afternoon and nothing's happening and I'm not going out in the evening, I just pick up my address book and phone friends for a chat. I do my garden, I play the piano, try to do some sports as well.

I think its very important to take exercise and so I swim. Keeping your body fit is extremely important. You feel so much better psychologically. But if you compound all the hard work and stress with: 'Oh my God, I've put on four extra pounds,' it doesn't help. I took myself in hand about a year ago and lost weight. I swam twice a week. That made a tremendous difference. I cycle as well and walk as much as possible.

I think it helps to have interests completely outside your profession. I feel sad for some of my colleagues who don't seem to have cultivated a life outside their political sphere.

My friends are very important to me. I'm lucky in that I have friends in theatre, film, TV, the arts; the areas outside politics that interest me. It's wonderful to get away and immerse yourself in something completely different; to put on a record, go to a concert or let music transport you away from it all.

It's also very important to take holidays and not to feel guilty about it. That's where I spend my money. Three or four weeks in the summer, a week at Christmas and Easter. I notice other colleagues not doing it and I think they are very silly because you quickly become stale and no good to anybody. You don't develop yourself or make new friendships.

Are you ever criticized?

Well . . . I am sometimes accused of not doing enough, but being an MEP is an impossible job. I represent nine constituencies and half a million people. It's completely crazy. Sometimes there is a lack of understanding towards what you are doing and trying to pack in and the number of calls that are made upon you. I have to operate at local level in and outside the party, at national level in and outside the party, and at European level in the same way in and outside my political grouping. The pressure is awful, aggravated by the fact there are so few women.

I am asked to give talks to various meetings because the MEP or MP is always asked first. They don't realize there are a great many other women qualified to speak on this, that or the other subject. They want the so-called important figure.

I get sick of being thought of as a political automaton on legs. That's another of the downs. I get home feeling that people have only looked at me for my ideas, and missed the human being altogether. That makes me very angry, especially working in a party that preaches brotherhood, sisterhood, compassion and caring. Sometimes I don't feel those elements are high enough on our own agenda.

How do you deal with criticism?

It depends what mood I am in. I am in a difficult position as a politician. I can't afford to alienate people. Perhaps I'm too much on the defensive sometimes. I once responded to an invitation to go on a Sunday anti-Cruise missile walk by saying I'm with you in spirit but not in body. I simply have to have time to myself. It was the first time I'd spoken about my need for personal space and, as I said before, my hope is that more men will start to do this and set limits. There's no evidence of it at the moment, but I believe it's important to be honest about why you are putting yourself first sometimes.

I was once accused of being a 'wild flower', meaning I didn't have a boyfriend, wasn't engaged and didn't look as if I was on the verge of getting married. My reply was 'chance would be a fine thing!' It's true. I feel there's no time in this job for meeting anyone, let alone developing a personal relationship. This honesty about my personal life sometimes throws people off guard.

You sound as if you find it easy to express your anger.

I make a fuss about things now that I wouldn't have done in the past, be it returning faulty goods, or tackling a government minister.

In common with female colleagues in my own and other parties, I get angry and frustrated when male colleagues turn up at meetings with a few notes on the back of an envelope. That shows complete contempt for the audience.

How do you maintain such a high level of self-confidence?

I sit down and think hard about what I am going to say, if not write a speech to prepare myself to say something meaningful, new and different. I am still scared of what may come out of my mouth, so, even now, after three years, I'll structure my contribution carefully, whether it's discussions with the CBI, a local school, the International Metalworkers' Federation or whatever. Within that framework, I think you make more sense than waffling on trying to think on your feet. It's a good sign, not being cocksure you've got all the answers.

In terms of the butterflies in your stomach, that's natural, healthy. Gradually they disappear. It took about a year in the job before the physical symptoms of nervousness went away. I started out with little self-confidence and built it up in the job. I believe you gain confidence by being thrown in at the deep end. Then there's no way out. You have to get on with it and produce the goods. It's amazing how well you can respond to that challenge.

Women might be quieter and not say much, but often when we do open our mouths we are likely to say something very worthwhile.

When do you feel vulnerable? How do you deal with it?

I can share my vulnerability with my female colleagues and check out how a speech went. I am able to show I didn't feel absolutely marvellous.

On a recent all-women campaign tour during the 1987 election, we had a ball! We barely had one dispute in four weeks; we each deferred to one another; we compared notes; decided who would do what; gave each other ammunition or advice on the way to put things across in a speech. There was no competition or drive for the limelight. I really felt I was in a sisterhood — it was fantastic! There's nothing to beat women coming up at a conference asking how you feel, how you are getting on and laughing about looking for the man of your dreams.

Being open about feeling vulnerable with male colleagues often leads to them telling you how intimidated *they* also feel at times. There are a number of male colleagues who have gone up in my estimation through showing vulnerability when so many won't.

Do you have a sense of your own spiritual needs, your own spirituality?

I am very much aware of my own spiritual needs. I miss not having someone as a soul mate, with whom I share a common philosophy and interests: listening to the same music or watching a TV programme and discussing it; enthusing about a book we've both read; someone who comes home with *their* day's experience and shares it with you.

I'm very much aware I need a bond with someone not a colleague at work and not in a material sense. I want someone who is fond of me because I'm me, not because I'm an MEP, and we can enjoy each other's company and share different things together.

I attend Quaker meetings and that has a profound effect on me. I call the Quaker tradition and beliefs the far left of non-conformism. Both my father and mother are Quakers. My mother influenced me particularly because I spent the bulk of my life with her. It's an egalitarian religion. There is no real discrimination against women or anyone else. There is an all-pervasive atmosphere of tolerance, understanding and co-operation. There is a desire to sit down and listen to what others have to say and bring conflicting attitudes to some kind of conclusion based on non-confrontation.

I find Quaker meetings very welcoming. I love the idea of questioning everything, never assuming the majority view is right, and never taking for granted that what seems to be the current ethos is necessarily the right one. Quakers are a group of people who try to live out their beliefs in their personal relationships and everyday lives, with a belief in humanity and a desire to improve the human condition. Attending Quaker meetings fulfils part of my spiritual needs.

Do you have a personal vision?

I feel British society is missing any response to people's spiritual needs. We are faced with very worrying trends in that only science and technology are considered important. For example, humanities and the arts take second place in the Tories' national core curriculum. There are fewer and fewer opportunities for people to express themselves in music, sport or art due to lack of funding or because funding is concentrated in one specific area.

I think the Church has an identity crisis. It speaks in a language which is irrelevant to most people nowadays. It could be argued the Labour movement is going through a similar crisis of identity and needs to reappraise the means by which it achieves its ideals and how it should best relate to the real experience of people out there.

What are you most proud of?

I am particularly proud of the relationship I can establish with people; that I am able to inspire enthusiasm, energy and courage, and that I don't alienate people. I'm proud of being able to juggle a very complex, full life, enjoy a lot of different things and explore different avenues in life. I'm proud of being able to play some part in resolving conflict. I'm pleased at coming away from a couple of difficult meetings and being told I was the blue helmet of the United Nations yet again! I'm proud of my capacity to get the most out of being thrown into any culture or any situation. I'm proud of having kept the number of friends I have, who are extremely loving, supportive, patient and loyal, and hopefully being able to offer them a lot. I'm proud of having had the courage to overcome absolute fear and terror of getting up and speaking in front of people, confronting things I've never confronted before, and making myself jump in the deep end and then being forced to swim.

Jane Lapotaire.

Jane Lapotaire

Actor

Jane reminded me we had met a long time ago. I was astonished that she remembered me, and it boosted my ego enormously! She welcomed me warmly into her home and we sat on either side of a huge pile of books which indicated she'd done almost as much research for the interview as I had.

Have you had specific goals and have they changed?

Yes and no! I wanted to be a writer but got side-tracked into acting at grammar school. I got Toad, in *Toad of Toad Hall,* but an attack of German measles which I pleaded would go unnoticed under my green make-up, put paid to my first role.

I shocked the establishment at school the following year by pushing forward a production of *Romeo and Juliet* with the boys' grammar school, next door. (It was a measure of the times — late 1950s — that we were never supposed to have any communication with the boys!) I played Juliet and I was lost, hook line and sinker — sunk! In my spare time, during A levels, I used to iron costumes for Ipswich Rep, and was told by my headmistress, to give up 'this juvenile obsession with the theatre' and do something sensible with my life, like go to university or be a teacher.

I wanted to go to university, but I wanted to be an actor more. Once I'd given up the idea of becoming a writer I wanted to be an actress with every fibre of my being.

I'm still trying to be a writer! I'm writing a book about my childhood with my foster mother, a remarkable lady called Grace

Chisnall. She fostered me at two months, when my mother left me, and she died recently aged 96. But, in a funny way, she's more in my life now than she was during the latter years of her life. I can talk to her, or rather if I shut up long enough I can hear her talk to me. She is the person I most admire, respect and wish to emulate. She was the only one who encouraged me to be an actress.

I've kept an essence of Gran, as I called her; her walking stick and her Methodist hymn book, which I wrote in when I was nine, and a blanket from her bed is now on mine.

When I got to drama school at 19 I thought to myself, 'If I'm not in a position five years from now to say, "I think I've made progress," then I'll get out.' At 24 I said the same thing again, but by then, and without realizing it, I had done very well. I'd gone from the Bristol Old Vic straight into Laurence Olivier's National Theatre. I was in work continuously for six years, but whenever I went home to Gran all she wanted to know was, 'When are you going to be on *Coronation Street*, then?' That taught me the futility of seeking people's approval as a gauge of personal achievement. I'm so pleased she was alive to see me win the Tony award for *Piaf*.

I never wanted to be famous or rich and I'm neither of those things. I didn't want to be typecast and I think I've maintained a large variety in the roles I've played. I haven't played on the fringe and I haven't done as much comedy as I would like, but I'm working on opening up those areas. My objectives and goals have been more than amply rewarded.

I go to university now — on a visiting Fellowship at Sussex. I take seminars of MA students in the Education Development section. Some of them have got two or three degrees. I'm terrified before each session, but I enjoy it enormously. I think, 'How can I fill two or three hours with what I know about acting, communicating or body language,' but they're so intelligent and stimulating. I learn such a lot and the time zaps by.

I still have a goal that's been rather badly battered over the years — to have a happy, stable, on-going relationship with a man. After my marriage to Rowan's father broke up, I had a goal to survive living alone. I think I've managed that. I enjoy my own company now. I didn't ten years ago.

Another goal, and I couldn't have said this ten years ago, is to *enjoy my life*. 'Enjoy' wasn't part of my vocabulary. My life was a struggle, a battle. Fun is a word I use more now.

I want to be a better gardener and a better watercolour painter.

I look forward to the book I've written about my foster mother being published, and people whose opinions I respect, perhaps saying, 'This woman can write.'

I am determined to have as varied a life as possible. I want very much to have another career, apart from acting. This first book being well received would encourage me to go on and finish my novel.

Theatre work is very demanding physically and I find, as I get older, that when a self-destructive, tragic, neurotic, unhappy role comes along, I ask myself, 'Do I really want to put myself through this again?' When I was young I would say 'yes' to any part that came along, especially as they got bigger. Now I'm more protective of myself: 'Do I really want to put myself on this unhappy trip?' And now, eight times out of ten I say 'No. I don't. I want to sit in my garden, read and write a bit. I don't want to have to dredge up all those negative experiences of myself in the past or put salt in those wounds. I want to relax a bit, enjoy my hobbies, go to the cinema more often, even manage to squeeze in a concert or an exhibition!'

Gaining a degree of self-esteem has been a battle I've fought for a long time. Like a lot of women, actors are typed according to how we look. Work has never come easily, particularly films or television parts where the physical aspect dominates. I'm not conventionally attractive; I don't have big boobs or a *retroussé* nose and, like most women, I've had to fight to keep a degree of self-respect in the face of daunting media brainwashing as to what an attractive woman is. But my unconventional looks have given me the chance to play some unique, strong, brave women: Marie Curie, Piaf, Eleanor of Aquitaine.

Have you been inspired by any of the characters you've played?

Playing women who lived is a very odd experience. By the time you've read every book on her life, looked at every photograph, painting, etc., you are probably walking as close to that other person's life as she herself walked. It's a very eerie feeling, especially if you play the character in the theatre, because then you have the chance of being with her for maybe six months, a year or, as in *Piaf*, for three years.

I believe when you play someone who lived you have a double obligation not to make any moral or value judgements. You can't allow your own values to make comments on hers, and you must honour that person and respect their beliefs even though they might not totally align themselves with yours. You can't stand outside that person and say, 'Look, this is what she did and felt.' That person must travel through you; you must open up every possible avenue about that person. It's like being a medium. It's opening up every single pore in your emotions, your mind, your spirit, your brain; allowing all this information to flow through you as freely as possible. You let it stew happily and then you start rehearsing the script. It's a process of osmosis; the coming together of *you* and *her*. I know this may sound a bit of a cliché, and I'm not apologizing in any way, but after my foster mother, Joan of Arc was the single biggest influence on my adult life, because she made me take stock of my own 'spiritual' beliefs and taught me to listen.

It will surprise you, but I played Joan of Arc when I was 40, and 14 to 16 were the most influential years of Joan's life. The more I read about her before I started rehearsal, the more I realized I couldn't play Joan without a 'faith', so I'd better work out what mine was.

Over the years I've picked up a rag bag of eclectic ideas about 'forces', energy and light, Jung's cosmos, the psyche, anima, animus, etc. Gran brought me up as a Methodist, and there were times when I went to the young people's service in the morning, Sunday school in the afternoon and church again in the evening. However, at 18, like many teenagers, I left the church, kept the collection money and went down to the local coffee bar for a frothy coffee or a Pepsi to eye the boys! By the last evening of playing Joan in England, in December 1985, my faith had become stronger and I prayed to have an enriching, developing relationship with what I believed it to be. By May 1987 my 'faith' — this inner belief — had become the central part of my life.

At the time I played Joan, Caroline, one of my dearest friends, had just survived breast cancer, was diagnosed as having cancer of the pancreas (there's a two per cent survival rate), and given just six months to live. Re-aligning and discovering my own inner beliefs became almost inextricably intertwined with some kind of positive form of thinking, or 'prayer' as I call it now, for Caroline. A month ago she was given the all-clear. They can't even find the bruise where the tumour was.

Joan of Arc wounded at the seige of Paris. Reproduced courtesy of Mary Evans Picture Library.

I've never prayed for anyone in my life as much as I prayed for Caroline. In the loo, in the middle of the night, in traffic jams, battling round the supermarket. I prayed for two years.

Part of my prayer took the form of dedicating many of my performances to her before I went on stage. I had been doing this for years, but before Joan or Caroline's illness it had been a habit, developed without any awareness of a link between the professional necessity of a focus for my evening's work, and a kind of inner belief. Often if a friend was in trouble, or ill, I would spend a few quiet moments of my warm-up session concentrating on that person and quite consciously dedicating a performance to the improvement of their situation. The piece of work then becomes an 'offering' which stops it being ego-bound.

I think on average I pray about 12 times a day. That's something I never did before I played Joan. I don't mean I get down on my knees and do it. But every morning before I open my eyes and start the day, I pray. Every night, too. Most people think praying is asking for things. Of course there are moments when I ask for things. I often ask for strength to face a day at work where my vulnerability has left me with less of my protective shell, or courage to face a darkness I have to journey through — and I get it.

The regained health of your friend Caroline must have enabled you to recognize the power of your inner energy, your prayer.

Yes, but cynics would say that for every friend who has prayed for someone to be saved from terminal cancer and been successful, there must be other people with a faith who've prayed and have not been successful. That's equally true.

Praying deeply for Caroline helped me understand the selfishness of my request for her life to continue, so that mine wouldn't be deprived of the pleasure she gives me. Consequently it helped me to understand that *whatever* the outcome, that's part of your journey, too. To have a faith is a paradox; there are no certainties and no guarantees. It's like a piece of music you've never heard before — it answers something in you. You *know* it, but the melody's not always clear.

Prayer is a very caring thing to do for yourself; it helps you take stock. Knowing what you need before you start the day helps you with the day. The problem isn't not getting what you want; it's knowing what it is you want in the first place, and making sure that you won't have to relinquish something essential to make space for this new 'request'. For me prayer helps define that question. It's very helpful to remind oneself there's an 'inner' life in this lunatic world of cut-throat greed, acquisitiveness and materialism.

Most orthodox religions are outward-looking, respectful of the individual's humanity, regardless of race, colour or walk of life. So, I think in a very general way it's important, politically, for some people to have a faith or inner relationship — be it Sikhism, Judaism or whatever. Mine's eclectic. It's not so much the talking as the listening which is the key to my spiritual experience and my faith. It's the difference between looking and really seeing — making the space to listen and trusting what you hear.

Faith will become of more and more importance as the external world is seen to be the empty shell that it is, when perceived in balance with an inner life. People will turn inwards more and more, and I think that is the only hope we have for the future. That private corner everyone has inside them is the only key to a better existence for us all, an existence without nuclear weapons and cut-throat greed. We've got our backs to the wall and I can't see any other way out.

Joan of Arc set me on the road to that realization. In the course of my character research, she made me think. I was left with a greater gift having played Joan than having played any of the other great women I've played.

Why?

Popular experience of Joan is limited because most of the plays about her are very pastoral, frilly and dated, and most of the historical records are prejudiced by the anti-Frenchness of the English, or doctored by the anger of the Roman Catholic Establishment. I believe there's a huge gap for a woman writer to do a play about St Joan; Bernard Shaw's St Joan isn't it. However much she fits into the Shavian idea of the 'new woman' — that she's unconventional, she wears men's clothes, she takes on the Establishment single-handedly — she is every contradiction of the stereotyped female; she was a military leader, a soldier, a knight, yet she was a peasant. (Although that's not strictly true; her father owned the land he farmed. He wasn't a tenant farmer.) In her 'hotline to God' Shaw lets Joan down badly. He had no room for faith in Joan, or for himself in the orthodox sense, yet she's a perfect example of *his* 'life force'. I think she would call that 'God'.

Because of his free-thinking attitudes and his total disparagement of orthodox religion, Shaw allows no time whatsoever for Joan to communicate to the audience that radiance, that quality of 'otherness' or that energy.

When I started working on the part I was interviewed by three women journalists on the trot, who, without even asking me what I thought of Joan's faith, made very disparaging and dismissive remarks about her being a schizophrenic, a psychopath, or psychologically disordered. I asked on what foundation they based their remarks. They had found it difficult to acknowledge the naivity of a person who possessed a total and all-absorbing, all encompassing belief in a faith that made saints appear in the garden to her. They were mistakenly comparing her to someone living in our modern, speedy, sophisticated world. It was simply her naivity that tipped the scales towards their seeing the woman as psychologically deranged.

I think Jesus Christ, and the saints, Margaret and Catherine, who spoke to her were her very real friends. Without being prissy, sentimental, precocious or sanctimonious, they fed her energy and commitment. Shaw's Joan fulfils every other obligation, but he parts company with her on religiousness.

The more I got to know Joan through the books I read on her life, and through a visit to Chinon, where Joan discovers the Dauphin for the first time, the link was doubled, the bond tightened, because my own mother was born only 50 kilometres from Chinon. Of course I've never had a spiritual experience on a par with Joan's and I doubt I ever shall, but that doesn't lessen my need or my conviction.

During the time I was researching and playing Joan there had to be a degree of real humility in that silent mental application before the show. I was dealing with someone who had dealt with 'God'. *I* had to deal with God. It gave me a sense of my place in the universe — both the smallness and the bigness of that place!

Part of my inheritance from Joan has lead me to read a great deal about religion. But, it's not easy and I'm still searching. I don't think of saints as such, or Jesus Christ even as the Son of God. Son of man, yes. I can't bring myself to recite the Nicene Creed and I find most orthodox religious services very difficult to stomach. They're an empty repetition, a tradition, not a celebration or joy or affirmation. Our priests nowadays are not even doctors of the soul anymore, let alone doctors of the body as the shamans are.

I was recently in a West End production and, as often happens to actors, was visited by the parish priest. I mischievously thought, 'Of the two of us, *he* would feel more embarrassed if I turned round and said, "Could we kneel down on my dressing room floor, and would you lead me in a prayer?"' I didn't, but I noticed he came into my dressing room clutching a thriller. He would have been surprised to hear what was inside my head, my performing a thriller at the time, yet also full of prayers.

It's always difficult to talk about spiritual beliefs because the language that we have is born of this existence which is a very tangible, palpable one. To describe spiritual experiences in modern language makes them either prosaic or banal or rather sanctimonious. I have to feel my way very carefully.

I think the choices are very clear cut and very few. It's either politics (socialism or capitalism, that is) or spirituality or materialism. I don't see how any person with a need for a spiritual faith in their life could be anything but left wing. It's the only philosophy that accounts for a very genuine care of people less privileged than oneself, or for whom life has not been kind.

There's no way I could be actively political; I'm far too emotional. I tried it when I was much younger, within Equity, the actors' trade union. I got far too passionate and carried away. Nothing ever got done because I was too busy waving my arms about, shouting and screaming. I was an embarrassment! My 'political activity' is now reduced to behind-the-scenes support for those groups to which I adhere philosophically and ethically. I could never be a card-carrying member of a political party because, again, this is linked to my developing spirituality bequeathed by Joan. I believe the greatest good is done between individuals by example, or by person-to-person commitment. I think people *en masse* are very frightening — emotions easily get out of hand. So, as politics was out, there didn't seem to be much else left but to get in touch with my spirituality.

When are you most vulnerable?

At work, during the 'osmosis process' and when I'm overtired — which I am most of the time! I push myself too hard. I overwork a lot. I'm better at taking days off and making time for myself now that my son is older and not so dependent, and now that

I've realized I don't have to be needed to be loved and I don't
have to 'do' to be loved — I can just be. But Blake was right, 'Energy
is Eternal delight!'

How do you cope with your vulnerability?

Not very well, but a lot better now than I did 10 years ago! I now
walk away from people who I find disruptive, or aggressive —
'vexatious to the spirit' — or who threaten my security. I 'perform'
to keep them at arm's length from what I'm really feeling. I haven't
developed a shell at all, other than removing myself from situations
that I recognize as dangerous. If you are brought up without family
security your need for approval and affection makes you
vulnerable. Although my foster mother gave me a kind of
constancy, she was old and I lived with the threat of her dying
and of what would happen to me if she did.

If you are open you are vulnerable, so to avoid being hurt you
mustn't be open. Unfortunately acting doesn't allow for that; being
open is part of the working process. I'm unable to keep things
at arm's length. If I'm hurt in my private life it goes straight in.
If I'm working I use that hurt to work with. I think — channel
it. In my worst moments I think, 'Remember the taste, the feel
of this. You might be asked to use it in a play!' I don't panic about
being vulnerable now; I can almost see it as an asset.

How do you take care of yourself?

I put aside time for *me* — time to rest, time to have fun. Like
a lot of women I'm very good at taking care of other people, but
god-awful at taking care of myself. I believe that's because women
are taught to be tray carriers. But I've learned to take care of myself
better, especially in practical ways such as putting my feet up in
the afternoons or spending a day at a women's health and fitness
centre in Covent Garden.

I've acquired middle-class standards and ideas about values on
leisure, too, because the success I have had with my work has
put me into a different class from the one I was born into. I've
learned to shut my own front door against the world and take
the phone off the hook, see no one and talk to no one. As an
actor who's lucky enough to work more often than not, I'm in
the public gaze, so my home is the burrow in which I hide and
heal. It was a revelation, when I bought this house. I didn't have

to consider anyone else's opinion about moving a picture or pot plant. Pottering about the house and garden always makes me feel better. I phone my women friends and have a good old natter, or I go to the cinema — it's such an escape — even though I know a camera arm or boom mike is only feet away from the shot. It still holds all the magic that I experienced as a child, when I stole money to go to Saturday morning pictures. I find now it's become vital for me at the end of the day to read some kind of book on spirituality. I've always dabbled in theology, but since Joan, I've a whole shelf of theological books upstairs.

Can you easily separate your public and private lives?

Very easily. I'm able to project an extrovert, energetic persona, but if you don't know me you won't get near me at all. I perform. I've had a bit of practise. I have a few close friends. I'm not a gregarious person, socially, at all. I tend to go with a girlfriend to the cinema, or have a girlfriend round here for dinner. When I'm on my own socially, I tend to be with people I feel safe with. The idea of going to a party and mingling in a room full of strangers is horrendous. I'll do it if it's a professional engagement — publicity for a play, or a theatre company obligation.

I am an intensely private person. I think it's largely to do with bringing up a son solo for nearly nine years, and when I'm preparing for a role but not actually rehearsing, I may not talk to anyone from 8 a.m. to 5 p.m., while my son's at school. Fortunately, my need for 'spirituality' gives me a sense that I'm not walking entirely alone.

What have been your highest moments?

Two instances stand out in my life. The first was going to Broadway with *Piaf* and winning the Tony Award. The other hugely important moment was my stepfather finally acknowledging I was successful.

Have you had to compromise in your career because you are a woman?

Oh God, yes! I've compromised because I'm a mother. I've had to provide a stable domestic environment in which my son could grow up without a father. That took precedence over career decisions when he was small.

I've chosen not to go away on location and film during term time; I've taken my son with me everywhere. He's 14 now, but when he was younger, if I couldn't take Rowan with me I didn't take the job.

I used to say to his father, 'We can talk about equality when you decide not to do a film job because you've not seen your son for three months.' That's not applicable just to him, it's applicable to most men with careers. There are a few brave souls breaking that convention by staying at home and looking after the children while the wife works, but they are still very few and far between.

There have also been professional compromises; for instance when I didn't find a particular script enriching or life-enhancing. Although I have never put my name on or myself into anything I disagreed with ethically or politically, I have done a load of one-dimensional, superficial rubbish, simply to pay the bills.

I've been self-supporting since 1979 and I've only owned my home since May 1983. Being a woman alone, having a mortgage and an endowment policy, meant the bank required me to have private sickness insurance and insurance to insure my salary. If I were a man living on my own I don't think I would be subjected to all those strictures. I have to make professional compromises to pay that kind of bill and to maintain a degree of domestic stability for Rowan, which I don't regret for a minute.

Have you made sacrifices?

Yes. I think I've sacrificed my relationships with men. The longer I live alone the more proprietorial I become about my home, and it's very difficult for any man to come in on an extremely close relationship between a mother and her son.

I also think women have set themselves up as mothers for their men. I've done it. I've said, 'Come to me, I'm Mrs Fix-it. I'll cook for you. You can put your head on my shoulder. I'll tell you what I think about the career decision you're facing,' and then when I'm feeling vulnerable and want to put my head on *his* shoulder — PANIC! The role and image of their woman changes and they can't cope.

But I'm learning. I was celibate for a long time, and I found it lonely not having another adult to share with at the end of the day. But I'm much less romantic about my relationships with men than I was 12 years ago. I'm not prepared to mother. I'm more secure in myself. That doesn't mean I'm always self-confident, but even on the days when I'm not confident I'm secure in the fact I'm just not confident *that* day and plan B takes over.

I demand an awful lot from myself and the man I'm involved with, and like many women running a family alone and a career, it does make you a little arrogant. I think we often see ourselves bordering on the Deity! We think, 'Poor baby, your BMW's broken down — but I'm having to make life-changing decisions about which school my son goes to next year; deal with his coming home from sport with a knee cap hanging half off; an Arabic friend he's invited home can't eat bacon for supper; my agent's just rung to say the TV series has just gone down the drain.' In the face of all that, engine failure tends to take second place!

The men I respect and really like have that very co-ordinated female side. They like women and are interested in us and our differences. I couldn't have a lasting relationship now with a man who didn't have a spiritual belief. But if I do have to grow older with my kitchen garden, my cats and my painting and writing, I would also like to grow old with a male soul-mate in the other armchair on the other side of the fireplace.

Has it been difficult to make yourself a priority? Your son is a priority. What about you?

That maternal thing is very strong in me. I am a coper, a fixer. I do have to work hard to make myself a priority in a relationship with a man, or on my own. Work takes priority when I'm on my own.

I have a phenomenal amount of energy; I tend to go at 150 rpm and then collapse, but now I enjoy collapsing. I'm proud of my energy — it may leave people gasping on the sidelines, but I love it. I never, ever sit around thinking, 'What shall I do next? The busy-ness stems from the fact Gran was 70 when I was 14, so I had to take on a great many practical responsibilities for the two of us when I was quite young. It's the working class, puritan ethic: work first play later — but by then you're too exhausted!

How do you cope with criticism?

It depends on the manner in which it is given. Professional criticism I can cope with reasonably well because it's part of the job, especially if it's given in a constructive, productive manner. You get notes after every rehearsal. Reviews I don't read. If they're good they kill future performances; by isolating a moment it dies for you. If they're bad they hurt. I read reviews after the last performance, then it's 'death where is thy sting?' It's only so much old fish and chip paper.

It's taken me 42 years to be able to admit that I'm a deeply sensitive person. What a cliché! A sensitive actor. My emotions are very near the surface all the time and personal criticism triggers a fear button.

I am not good about personal criticism. It activates the frightened negative little girl in me. Also, it worries me that not only have I failed to acknowledge something about my own personality which is evident to somebody else, but somehow their knowing that something about me I hadn't been aware of means they've got one over on me!

If the criticism comes from someone I love and respect who loves me, I'll probably resent it like mad at first and shout about it, then I'll go away and mull it over. If, after that, I think they're right, I'll try to do something about it.

What are the things you are most proud of?

My son. I'm very proud of my son. I brought him up with a rod of iron! In our house there are three rules: eat up, shut up and hurry up. Don't muck about; if it's bed, it's bed. If you muck about I can't learn my lines and I'll be dreadful at rehearsal tomorrow, and maybe the director won't use me again. You've got your choice: live with me as a friend and I'll treat you as a friend. I'll knock on your door and not assume that because I'm your mother I have a right over your property or your time.

I'm very proud when people meet him and say what a lovely boy he is. I'm proud of him because he is self-contained and has a degree of self-assurance at 14 I didn't have at 34. I am proud that he is his own person and I am proud that I've done it virtually alone. Yes, I'll take that credit.

I'm also very proud I'm *me*. I never thought that I'd be able to say that. I'm proud of feeling comfortable inside my own skin.

Not all the time, but I'm proud of being able to get through the times when I don't feel comfortable inside my skin.

I'm proud when someone says 'Jane Lapotaire, we are very pleased to have you here being part of this meeting.'

I'm proud when someone treats me with respect. I think, 'Golly, I must have earned that!'

I'm proud that I'm living on my own and that I can do it. If somebody had waved a magic wand 10 years ago and said, 'Jane, you're going to live on your own,' I think I would have done something very serious to myself. I was so frightened of facing myself. I think I would have done anything rather than live on my own.

I'm proud I can now do some of those little jobs around the house that I was terrified of because there wasn't a man to do them. I'm proud I can mend a fuse, wire a plug. I'm proud I re-tiled the bathroom.

I'm proud that, not being a singer, I had the sheer blatant *chutzpah* to stand up on stage and convince people I could sing, when deep down inside I knew I couldn't.

Actually, I am proud of *Piaf* in a way the audience wouldn't understand. I met one of the supporting actors recently, Anthony Higgins — he's a big film star now — and he said, 'That production of *Piaf* was the happiest time I ever had in the theatre.' I remember I quite consciously tried to lead that company in a very positive way; I put almost as much energy into what went on backstage as on stage.

It was very difficult for the men because they were playing the ciphers — small walk-on parts. The boot was on the other foot for once. It was the women, and Piaf mostly, who had the lioness's share. So for that man to say, six years after the event, that I, together with Howard Davis the director, was responsible for the happiest production he'd been involved in, makes me proud.

And I'm very proud of my watercolour paintings.

How do you cope with your failures?

Badly. They are a stick with which I constantly beat myself. I'm a perfectionist, and very hard on myself.

If one of my plants die, I think, 'What did I do wrong?' But Glad, my next-door-neighbour, who's a green-fingered old age pensioner, pops her head over the fence and says, 'I've just dug

up all those bulbs I got from Marks. They weren't very good this
year were they?'

Women still think being successful professionally will mean
your private life suffers, which of course it does. Work, children
have priority — there are only 24 hours in a day — the men get
what's left over. But they've been giving us those kind of left-
overs for years.

I saw an American businesswoman on TV recently, who was
asked about her love life. She replied it was non-existent. 'When
I succeeded professionally it went. Successful women frighten
men.'

Don't you think it's unfair?

Well, of course, but whoever believed life was fair? Anyway,
women want it all, don't we?

But why doesn't it happen to men?

Because men have wives! Also, I think the male sexuality is linked
with ego and women's sexuality isn't. That is, if he's successful
he's sexually attractive. If *she's* successful, she's a ball-breaker.

I think the sexual side of women's ego is bound up with her
biology, which has a nurturing function.

Like men, we have a need to excel in our professions, but I
know of no relationships within my immediate social circle where
both the man and the women are comparably successful. In every
case except one, it is the woman who has taken the back seat,
professionally. Men get undermined by women earning more than
they do. That's why it's very difficult for a successful female actor
to have a relationship with a male actor who is not as successful.

Some women tend to be as irrational about failures or
shortcomings as we are about our good qualities. The truth is
somewhere in between. It's only by allowing yourself to
acknowledge those shortcomings in a rational, unexaggerated way,
that you can then establish a healthy assessment of what your
good qualities are. The pendulum swings from one extreme to
the other less and less. The bad things and the good things are
aligned.

If you asked me my biggest failure professionally, I'd be hard
put to answer. There's been something gained, something learned
from every job. My girlfriends tell me I've always been very shrewd

in my work. I have to know exactly why it is I'm doing a particular job. There are jobs to pay the bills, jobs that are enriching, challenging. There are jobs that are fun, silly. There are jobs I'm not passionate about but I'd like to work in that set-up with that particular director.

I have jobs which have not been a success in the public's eye, but I know I've done them to the best of my ability. For every five people that say, 'That was a load of rubbish, there are another five who say, 'I don't know why that didn't run and run, it was wonderful.'

Professionally, I am very subjective about what a certain role can offer me and what the director will do as far as pushing back the horizons of any limitation is concerned. I do get cross with myself when I know a particular director's limitations, but even then he manages to block me. There's nothing worse than doing a job for the best possible reasons and ultimately having to admit that you've been blocked at every turn and nothing except your own inability to handle the shortcomings of the situation is to blame.

I feel I've failed if I sink into the old, 'You're no good, Jane.' I have to remember that's not part of my life now. I'm not frightened of myself anymore, so maybe that has something to do with not being frightened of public failure. I'm not proving anything to myself anymore.

All credit goes to Rowan's father. When I was lying in bed with sweat trickling down my forehead in cold fear, awash with insecurity about whether I had bitten off more than I could chew with *Piaf*, afraid I was going to meet my Waterloo in a very messy, public way he said, 'There's nobody better qualified in England to play this role than you. Your mother is French, you understand where Piaf came from because of your English background.' And for the first time in my working life I believed I had a right to walk on stage, a right to be on this earth, a right to be here. I was 34.

I would deem it enormous failure if I had actually taken on a branch of acting in which I had absolutely no experience, singing, for example, and not learned how to do it properly.

I worked at Covent Garden Opera House with a singing teacher for six months before we even went into rehearsals. There was no way I was going to take the part of a singer and be off with vocal trouble, and for three years I never was, even on Broadway with seven shows a week.

I remember there was an article in the *Sunday Times* colour

supplement not long after I'd opened in *Piaf.* Lord Snowdon and
David Bailey were invited to take pictures of the most promising
actresses, and I cried because I was not one of the seven. It wasn't
just because I hadn't been included, but I knew I had reached
the limit of my potential as an actress. I couldn't have done another
15 minutes of that play. I couldn't have done another song. I could
do two-and-a-half hours and sing eight songs, but that was my
limit and I had not reached those limits before. I thought if *they*
want more than that then I don't have it to give and that was what
made me unhappy.

What makes you laugh, get angry, sad?

The yob culture makes me angry. People's disregard for each other;
lack of politeness; selfish drivers, someone who drives
inconsiderately or dangerously. The lack of grace in the world
makes me sad. I'm not good at getting angry, I'm an oil-on-
troubled-waters lady.

It's a red rag to a bull when my son won't admit that he's wrong,
because it's my own personal dirty washing in my face. I would
do anything as a child to get out of confronting the fact I had
made a mistake. I've learned through having Rowan that I can
be wrong.

I've come to laughing late in life. Lunacy makes me laugh. I
love Monty Python, John Cleese's Ministry of Funny Walks —
it's insane — Richard Pryor, Bette Midler. I love a healthy dose
of vulgarity. I like Billy Connolly — that's because I had a Scottish
boyfriend once, so I was let in on those Scottish bits. Left to my
own devices, I'm a rather serious, introspective person. Humour
doesn't play a large part in my life when I'm on my own.

Fellowship with women makes me laugh. I laugh more easily
with my women friends. I can be a fool, clown to make someone
feel better. Socially, I can be as hilarious and gregarious as the
next person, in fact, two of my close actress friends and I have
emptied many a restaurant with our raucous guffaws.

My son makes me laugh a lot. Together, at half past 11 at night,
illicitly dumping stuff in other people's skips.

I like Dave Allen because he's a social satirist. His comedy is
born of the here and now of the world.

Ruby Wax makes me laugh, she's so outrageous and vulgar,
blasting all the conventions about women.

But, in the BBC Bookshop, faced with a copy of *Yes, Minister* and Gerald Priestland on religion, I'd opt for Gerald Priestland every time.

What's the lesson that you are most glad to have learned?

That I have a right to walk the earth. That I can accept that I am good and bad and not want to be somebody else. Over and above that, that life is a gift, a journey. It isn't a rehearsal; this is it. That no meeting, no friendship is without meaning. I can't answer for what happens after this, but I know the spirit and the soul don't disappear; the body is just a casing for it.

I'll always treasure a remark my son made as an explanation of misdemeanour. 'But, I've never been anyone's son before.' I never had a role model for mother or father, so bringing up my son on my own really has been a journey without signposts. I had to watch girlfriends with families and learn continually, measuring my own experience of being a parent against theirs. I am grateful to all those people I watched. My son taught me I could be wrong, make a mistake.

Do you have a personal vision of how you would like the world to be?

I pray for peace and more compassion between people. The cruelty in the world saddens me incredibly, not least of all because I have a child. Nuclear war is something I rarely get through a day without thinking about. I would like a world where people matter because of what they are, not what they have. I would like to see a world where the world matters. What have we done to the earth in the pursuit of money? I would like us all to love ourselves, *really* love ourselves and consequently love each other more.

One of the relevations in my life is women. Women in touch with their intuition and integrity hold all the cards.

I would never have thought when I was a teenager, and extremely competitive regarding other girls, that I would ever, ever, count women as my first priority, over and above men. They gave me tremendous support during the early days of being a mum. Like a lot of young mums I thought it was *my* inadequacy that made me want to throw the baby against the wall. It wasn't wet or hungry, so why in God's name was it still screaming its

head off? It was just the pressure of living in a nuclear family and
being on my own all day trying to cope with shopping, London
traffic, and all the rest of it. I find great support and comfort from
my women friends. I think we take that kind of female support
and comfort for granted now. In fact, when you meet a 'man's
woman', one that doesn't like other women, you think, 'Golly,
she's a bit odd!'

I think it's remarkable that nowadays, in spite of our
conditioning, fewer women compete with each other in that way.

I would like to see a world where feminism isn't, and isn't seen
to be, devisive; where men and women work and walk hand in
hand as *people*; a world where religion isn't used as an excuse
for war or a disguise for power; a world where the inner life is
given as much importance as the outer.

Liz Hodges sitting in a Wessex helicopter belonging to the Search and Rescue of HMS Daedalus. *Photograph by H. Amlivvala. Reproduced courtesy of the photographic section of* HMS Daedalus. *Crown copyright.*

Liz Hodges

Surgeon Commander, Royal Navy

Liz Hodges is the first woman in the Royal Navy to be granted a full career commission and the first British woman to have completed the Diploma in Aviation Medicine at the Royal Aircraft Establishment (RAE) at Farnborough and now she is the first woman promoted to the rank of Surgeon Commander in the Navy. She has taken up the post of President of the Central Air Medical Board and is Medical Officer in Charge of the Royal Naval Air Medical School at the Royal Naval Establishment, Seafield Park, Fareham — an out-station of HMS Daedalus.

I caught sight of the pilot's overalls and helmet hanging behind the door as I settled down to begin the interview.

What or who was the motivation for doing what you are doing now?

The whole time I was at Cambridge and the London Hospital my sister was going out with a naval officer, whom she's since married. I was invited to lots of social functions and learned how the Navy operates. I come from a non-service family; Father was a GP. I saw the Navy enjoy themselves and when they are not enjoying themselves they work very hard. That 'work hard, play hard' routine suits me.

I do enjoy myself, I love sports, travelling and socializing, but when I'm at work I like to be kept busy. I don't like sitting around twiddling my thumbs all day.

At that stage (1977) I had no idea there were female doctors in the Navy. I thought the Navy was totally male, apart from the Wrens, and I knew the Wrens didn't recruit doctors or dentists.

I met a Navy dentist who said his wife was a Navy doctor. I

fixed up an appointment to see her and she showed me what
she did and chatted to me. I submitted an application form and
six months later I was in. It was just something I fell for straight
away and I suppose they fell for me! But my original ambition,
whilst going through house jobs at the London Hospital, was to
become a general surgeon. I knew the way ahead for me was
going to be very hard, because at the time I was told there were
only two women in the UK who were consultants in general
surgery. One was a spinster in her 50s, the other married with
loads of kids. I don't know how she managed to do it. I was
motivated by the fact that at least two women had made it. I wasn't
sure I'd make a consultant, but there was a door open to women
in surgery.

What encouraged you to continue with that ambition?

My love for surgery. I love needlework, using my hands and, of
course, the brain has to function quickly too!

The first six months of my house job year was in surgery,
at a hospital just outside London, under a rather chauvinistic
surgeon. But within weeks of working for him, we somehow
clicked. He taught me general surgery and his other major interest
— arterial surgery. I used to assist him during four and five hour
operations and he taught me as we operated. We got on very,
very well and he wrote me a superb reference when I left. I
suppose I was motivated by the fact that such a male chauvinist
had been able to spot my talents — my ability to work hard,
use common sense, be a good communicator and make neat
incisions!

Surgical emergencies suited my personality down to the
ground. You examine a patient, decide what tests to do, do them
at the time and then you decide whether or not to operate. Many
surgical emergencies are not operated upon. We treat
conservatively, but, when you do decide to operate, the patient
is anaesthetized and you can't hop off to consult a book or close
them up and open them up the next day when you've decided
what to do. You make decisions on the spot. I enjoy thinking
on my feet and seeing the end product of my work immediately.
I get great job satisfaction from that.

What about the myth of tremendous physical stamina being required of surgeons?

It's true; that is essential. You need to be a fast worker. It's changed now because the number of hours you were on duty meant you could be a potential danger to patients, but when I was a houseman (1978) you had to be capable of being on call for 140 hours a week, probably 120 of them actually on your feet! Not one night on duty went by without me being phoned or called out. Once was a Godsend, but it was usually two or three times each night. I got into a routine of waking immediately and returning to sleep immediately. If you had been up all night you couldn't take the morning off. You had to work right through the day as well until five or six that evening.

Physical strength is needed to hold a couple of retractors at an operation. A retractor is the metal instrument that holds back skin, muscles, organs, etc., so that you have a clear view of what you are doing and ample space to work in.

How did you achieve that fitness?

I row. I rowed at Cambridge and for London University Women, and for the hospital, but not in my house jobs because I was too busy, and that made me very fit.

At the London Hospital there were four flights of stairs between my wards. I never took the lift.

You have to be emotionally strong too, because there were times when you were so tired you had to kick yourself into waking up and carrying on.

In spite of the pressure I never had one morning when I thought to myself, 'God, I simply can't get out of bed today.' It was so very satisfying. I worked with many terminally ill cancer patients, some of whom died in my presence. They had an enormous sense of a belief in life, even if they didn't believe in God. They imparted something to me. When you are that close it gives you the will to carry on yourself. Whenever I get a bad cold I always consider myself to be fit and healthy.

I spent six months doing my surgical house job and six months doing the medical house job, three months of which was in casualty, and three months of which was general medicine and radiotherapy. Casualty required 10 hour shifts. I saw alcoholics, battered wives, gun wounds, knifings, psychiatric cases. That was very exciting, but often very sad.

What kept you going?

There was always something new coming in. Because it was so
busy there was no time to sit and think. In some ways that's bad,
because as a junior doctor you need to consolidate what you've
just learned and often there was no time for that. There was always
something exciting going on. There'd be a lull, then suddenly
the police would rush in with an ambulance case — a girl with
multiple knife wounds, screaming. She sees another female and
wants to talk; you sit there alone with someone threatening to
kill you. Or an Oxford don arrives, feeling a bit unhappy,
threatening to jump of London Bridge — all he wants is someone
to talk to; or a Pakistani comes in — he's been shot from a passing
car while out walking, and a dart from an airgun pins his upper
eyelid to the orbital ridge above his eye. Someone arrives from
a building site with a severed hand. I loved the blood and gore!
I never minded having a go at something. Being with people less
fortunate than yourself makes you more content with your own
lot. Your own problems become minor ones and they motivate
you to carry on.

Did you have the support of your family during this time?

Absolutely. I've never been pushed. My parents are very proud
of their children. My sister's a barrister, married with a child. Daddy
always says, 'Aim high but don't be disappointed if you don't
make it.'

Have you ever experienced failure and how did you manage it?

My sister and I both failed our professional exams first time round
and it made my parents realize that their two bright daughters
were only human. Failing can bring an element of modesty into
what you know is an above-average brain. The lowest point of
my life was failing my surgery exams on one small part: a 15-minute
viva [oral exam].

That failure knocked me off my pedestal, but it was the best
thing that could have happened to me. Up till then I thought I
was God's gift to surgery. Failing knocked me into touch, brought
me down to earth and made me take a good long look at myself.

No-one could understand me failing a subject I was so good at, but I wasn't deterred; I simply waited another six months and re-sat the surgery.

Then what happened?

Having decided to join the Navy to work hard and play hard, I went to see my boss at the time to ask if I could leave a week early and join. He said I was wasting my time. He thought that the Navy didn't offer good career prospects for doctors. He actually threatened not to release me from my last week because he thought I was wasting a very promising career. I managed to talk him round, have met him since and he's absolutely thrilled with the progress I've made.

In the Navy at last, my first few weeks' introductory course entailed learning to march, how to be a Naval officer and learning about Naval medicine. I then had to be interviewed by the professor of surgery because I wished to pursue my surgical career.

I had been informed at my initial interview the Navy doesn't promise to train you in anything, but they do their best to train you in whatever you want. However you occasionally get caught up in the 'numbers game': too many people in one subject, not enough in others. That's when persuasion comes in.

That year there were two candidates: myself and a male, competing for the one place on the training scheme. The man, a friend of mine, said there was no point whatsoever in my trying because he was sure to get it because he was male! Fortunately they agreed to interview both of us.

The professor of surgery was very much a man's man, with a great deal of common sense and heart. He was terribly fair. I got the usual question: 'Why should we start you on a training course when you might get married, go off and have babies?' I replied: 'I wish to have a career and then think about getting married and having babies. Please give me the chance.' He appeared so chauvinistic, I couldn't believe it when he actually agreed to train both of us.

It's not surprising that some men think this way, as an awful lot of women doctors give up their careers to have a family and never return to medicine thus 'wasting' their training.

In the Navy you must complete two years' general medical duty before being trained in a speciality. The delay makes no real difference to your career. I was sent to the Royal Naval Air Station at Yeovilton. While there I asked to do a correspondence course for my primary examination in surgery and the Navy agreed to pay for the course. I completed it but didn't carry on with surgery because I realized during that first year that maybe there was something else I could do, and maybe I was a little blinkered having decided to do surgery and that's all.

I had discovered something that interested me a great deal and appeared to be within my reach. I had developed an intense interest in aviation medicine. I used my femininity to the best advantage. I got airborne in anything offered, including the Historic Flight, i.e. the Swordfish, Firefly and Sea Fury, in spite of a long waiting list. The boss needed a medical and in return I was given a flight. I learned about aircraft, sat and chatted with the crew and found I had a fascination for aviation medicine.

Aviation medicine combines everything from clinical medicine to psychology. A pilot develops hypertension — does he fly? If so, in what medical category? A pilot with a cold — does he get airborne today, or next week? On the psychological side, there are the aptitude and personality tests. What happens if a pilot develops a fear of flying? Why has he developed this fear? Is it an innate problem within his personality, or the result of an awkward approach to his ship at night, or being shot at in the Falklands? Perhaps it's pressure from home.

Aviation medicine also encompasses environmental problems, i.e. low oxygen pressure, visual problems, decompression sickness, disorientation, etc. It includes design of cockpits, life-rafts, ejection seats, first-aid kits for aircrew, and so on. It also covers cockpit ergonomics.

For example, an ejection seat has to be designed for a new aircraft. You've the old designs to work with. You've got the combined problem of the pilot's ejection, plus the need for him to sit comfortably in a seat for hours on a sortie. Where do you put the instruments? The decision requires a logical, commonsense approach to the problem and that's what I have.

Then there's the civilian side: airport health, zoonosis, time-zone changes, tropical diseases, and airport health authority laws.

I found my interest in surgery could be projected laterally into aviation medicine. It's interesting in that we still don't know everything about it, so I can still apply my medical brain and my personality to the same subject.

I got an enormous thrill out of getting airborne. The first time I got into a Hunter aircraft, a fixed-wing fighter trainer, was after

I had been to the site of a crash, where I picked up two pilots who had ejected from a Hunter. One had a broken back; one was OK. The broken back recovered. Funnily enough that motivated me to get airborne. I saw the minimal problems you can have with ejecting if you're lucky enough to have time to pull the handle.

I'm excited by flying. I've done a 42-hour flying course (with the Navy), but the three hours solo was an effort; I was glad to get back to the airfield! I've been over the Snowdonia mountain range in a Hunter, flying in and out of ravines and gorges, four to five G pulling your face down to your feet. You feel as if you're about to black out because there's so much G. The rocks coming towards you — its incredible! The pilot. Without that faith in him, I'd have hated every minute. I think if my time comes to go, my time is up. I don't fear death, illness or being maimed. At the same time I rather enjoy life and being fit and healthy. I'm a fatalist.

What's it like being in an almost exclusively male environment?

Air crew love new baby female doctors. With 10 female officers and 250 men at a base they adore having a new bird on the scene. But whether they would come to you for a medical or not was debatable. The fact I could do medicals, was an open sort of person, and 'mucked in' meant they eventually asked to have their medical done by me, because they knew I was thorough. Air crew may joke about things, but being fit is very important to them and they feel they get a good deal from me. My approach to men who may be embarrassed at having to strip down to their pants is: don't give them time to be shocked. By the time they're down to their underpants I'm well into taking their medical history and they've become quite relaxed. In any event, with the increase in women GPs many men are used to being examined by a female doctor.

A while ago I did my flying course in a Bulldog. You must wear a parachute. I'm five feet, two inches. There I am, the first Navy girl to go through on this service course. I walk out. Well, I'm like a snail with a shell on my back. Everyone's laughing and I laugh with them. As far as I'm concerned there's even a humorous side to sexual harrassment. Women put up with sexual harrassment all the time in the Navy. At a mess dinner I might be the only female. We all enjoy a drink. At the end of the evening

some of the chaps are a little more liberal with their comments
than they ought to be. I don't turn round and say, 'How dare you!'
My attitude is, fine, how charming — he's decided I'm the apple
of his eye at that moment. It's not what I want because I think
he ought to go home to his wife, or I can't stand him and don't
fancy him! I'll manoeuvre him into another corner, without him
realizing it. I can then escape from a potentially embarrassing
situation. I'll probably get a phone call the next day saying, 'Sorry,
Liz. I think I was a bit rude to you, forcing my attentions on you.'
I'll reply, 'Thanks very much for phoning up. Forget it, but don't
do it again!' The only time anyone has put a hand on my backside
was my flying instructor. I had difficulty clambering on to the
aircraft wing and then into the cockpit. I said, 'Thanks very much.
I'll find another way of getting in next time.'

I do search and rescue in helicopters but not much now. Once,
on a training exercise, instead of winching me straight back up
the guys in the helicopter knew I was on the end of the winch
and winched me half way. The pilot flew off and there I was,
50 feet off the end of a winch wire, speeding along above the
water. They did it to frighten me but they knew I wouldn't mind
too much. Safely on board I retaliated by saying, 'Wait till you
come for your medical! Watch out; cold hands . . .' This is a male
environment. You must enjoy being with men. You have to ignore
the male jokes and childishness, the male attitude towards you.

You play a crucial role in keeping them
airborne, don't you?

I believe in trying to bridge the gap between doctors and aircrew.
They are constantly worried that you'll ground them — stop them
flying. They can see me as a doctor wanting to know exactly what
their job entails, rather than someone simply looking after their
health. That bridge is vital because it's my job to decide their
futures if they sustain an injury or develop an illness. I need to
know the different aircraft roles and skills required when flying
a Lynx helicopter solo or being part of a Sea King helicopter team.
If you're on treatment such as certain antihypertensive treatments
which relax you to the extent you may not be able to react
properly in emergencies, you are still fit to fly, but not solo —
you can only fly with another pilot. So, Lynx is out, but Sea King
is a possibility.

I try as often as possible to get out and about and learn exactly what my aviators do. I believe it helps them decide to come and see me if they have a medical problem. They know I won't ground them unless it's absolutely necessary. I'm a friend, not an alien.

I recently took part in three three-hour helicopter sorties from *HMS Illustrious,* flying at sea. Land was 100 miles away. It was fascinating experiencing the tedium of hovering 50 feet above waves, for 10 minutes. You press a button and the aircraft hovers for you all by itself. Yet those pilots must be motivated and alert enough to react instantly if the automatic equipment or anything else suddenly goes wrong.

What helped you move on?

In 1980, after two years at Yeovilton, I was invited to go to the Institute of Aviation Medicine at Farnborough and take the Diploma in Aviation Medicine. I was the first British lady doctor to do it. There are only 12 or 14 places each year; amost half of those places go to foreigners. The majority of the remaining places go to the RAF and there's one place for the Navy and one for the Army.

That year, the Navy didn't have anyone interested. Obviously they wanted to keep the seat warm and, as I had spent a year at an air station, and showed such an interest in flying, they offered me the place. I was in the right place, at the right time. Fortunately that has happened throughout my career. I sit back, watch things go by and grab what I want. It's no good waiting for things to come to you.

What are your current goals?

Right now, I'm in an awkward position. No-one expected me to get this far so quickly, and I didn't set out to get where I am. The more senior you become in the forces, the more likely you are to end up in a desk job. My particular personality requires me to be with people. It would cripple me if I had to sit up in London doing a desk job, deciding on medical provisions for ships at sea during war.

I've met with a lot of male chauvinism on the way up. There were problems with my present position. I was told that since I was female, I didn't understand male aviators' problems; I hadn't been to sea and therefore I couldn't understand aviators' problems at sea. But it wasn't my fault that women are not allowed to go to sea in 'fighting' ships. They completely ignored the fact I had spent two years at Devonport dockyard, Plymouth, looking after dockies and clambering over every ship, submarine, tug, barge, fleet auxiliary ship, or whatever, so as to understand clearly from first-hand experience the working conditions of my patients. Or how I overcame the fact I hadn't been to sea by projecting my imagination so as to assess the possibility of a chief stoker returning to work with, say, a badly sprained ankle. That had been very demanding mentally. I had had to make a positive effort to go out and get that first-hand experience; no-one suggested I do it. I could have spent those two years just sitting in my office.

I felt they were questioning my medical judgement. My pride took a severe knock. At that point I thought about doing something very dramatic and resigning. I thought, 'What's the next best thing I can do?' A few very supportive male colleagues said, 'Just go and do the job and prove yourself.' I said, 'You don't understand how difficult that is. I've been proving myself to men for the last 16 years. I don't see why I should still be proving myself at this stage. However, if that's what it's going to take, I'll have to do it.'

Apart from failing my medical finals first time round, that was the biggest knock. I really thought I couldn't go on competing with the men at a higher level any more. My efforts were rewarded by a particularly chauvinistic officer changing his mind about me. He saw what I was able to achieve and finally gave in to the fact that some women do have a place in a male environment. After 18 months into the post, I've apparently proved myself. I have recently been made a consultant in occupational medicine with aviation medicine as my sub-speciality and I have spent five days at sea in a Royal Navy 'fighting' ship. I owe a lot to the people who made that possible.

To most men in the Navy, women are there to provide services. They do secretarial and staff jobs. Naval men fear women's success as it opens the floodgates. They fail to appreciate that most women want neither the responsibility nor the constant battle. However, my example could attract those women with the right motivation, skills and personality to enter an interesting career.

Colleagues joke about the fact I might be the first female Admiral. Maybe I will, but occasionally I ask myself how many more challenges I can successfully take on. Then before I've the chance to sit and think too hard about it another project drops on my desk, the phone rings, someone asks for help with a difficult case and suddenly I've dealt with everything without realizing the increase in workload.

I don't wish to think too much about where I go from here because of the fear of ending up behind a desk. I prefer being with people. Perhaps I will find my niche in a desk job. I'm open minded about it. I think if I can cope with this job, I can cope with anything.

What sacrifices have you had to make?

The emotional side to my life; having a relationship that would have developed into marriage. So far the men in my life have either wanted me to marry but leave the service, and not understood I don't want to leave just yet, or wanted us to marry, for me to stay in the Navy, be the first female Captain and not have kids because he has them from a previous marriage. Then I think, 'Oh, but I'm at a stage in my career when I could actually leave. And maybe I want my own kids and to be settled; sit at home making jam; do part-time medical work; be like other women.'

I'll always have to work. I couldn't not practise medicine. I've not met the right man at the right time. Men see me either as a housewife with children or progressing even further in the Navy (which means no housework or children). They just don't see me as a wife *and* mother who practises medicine!

When the man of the moment leaves the scene it's pretty upsetting. But my attitude is, there's always someone else round the corner. Get on with life and don't sit back and mope. I'm very much a present-day person; mistakes in the past I put behind me.

This week I had a telephone conversation with the man of the moment. I wasn't particularly inspired and I thought, 'Am I pursuing the right man? Should I be putting as much effort into this relationship as I am?' I felt tired. I couldn't cope with it. I wanted someone to talk to and there wasn't anyone suitable around, so I put my track suit on and ran for an hour round the housing estate, along the sea front. I got back home, absolutely exhausted, fell into a bath and lay there thinking, 'Phew . . . Right. Now. I wonder what book I'll read tonight before I go to sleep. Tomorrow's another day. Hang on in there; take things bit by bit. Don't make a decision tonight.'

It takes it out of me. I feel emotionally exhausted but I have to motivate myself in that way, because my responsibilities at work mean I cannot allow my emotional problems to take over. I must set them to one side.

How do you nurture yourself and put yourself first?

I give myself treats and justify them to salve my conscience. For my birthday I will always buy myself a super present — something I really want. I give so much of myself to my patients that now and then I need to take.

My holidays. I spend a lot of my salary travelling. I have few commitments: a mortgage and a car. I don't enjoy being a woman; vulnerable, alone in a resort. But then it's better than going on holiday with the wrong person. I have very few female friends. Most of them are married now. I tend to go on exotic, exciting holidays like safaris or to India. I was there when Mrs Ghandi was assassinated. I love seeing the way other people live. Lying on the beach all week isn't my scene.

When I'm invited to a ball there's no-one to say, 'Sorry, there's no money. You'll have to wear what you wore last year.' I can spend what I can afford. I'm not restricted by the man's budget. I'm going to have to face up to the lack of independence that goes with marriage and I'll do it when the time comes. Until then I'll spoil myself because there's no-one around to do it for me.

Has anyone inspired you?

In recent times, my sister, in that while she was pushing herself through Bar exams, I was pushing myself through medical exams. We gave each other support. Being so close, we always helped each other. Even the men we chose were different, so there was no sexual rivalry either.

If my school friends saw me now they wouldn't recognize me. I was a very quiet, studious, dowdy little girl. My sister was the opposite. She was pretty, frivolous, very intelligent but only worked at what she wanted to do. Our roles have switched. She has now become the serious one in the family; I'm the joke. My sister interests them; I make them laugh. There's only a year between us. She's happily married, has a five-year-old son and is super at her job. In some ways, I think she's achieved more than I have.

What are the positive aspects of being a woman in your job as Surgeon Commander?

Persuasion. I persuade people around me to give me what I want.
Generally I think women have more common sense. They tend
to be more logical and methodical. In this job I have generated
more work than perhaps my predecessors and I cope with it
because I am methodical.

I possess common sense and a very practical mind. I approach
my job in a practical, methodical way, perhaps because I was
brought up to make beds and wash up efficiently. I may have
a lot of paperwork to tackle at the end of a busy day, but I'm
not flustered. I think men approach their work in a slightly more
chaotic manner.

Being a woman in my job, the emotional drain focuses on
coping with the supervising of a team of men, whereas a man
doing this job would find the emotional drain focusing on
completion of his paperwork in a logical manner.

I think Navy men are learning to appreciate their female
colleagues because we show ourselves to be emotionally more
stable.

I try to work according to how people react to me. I am able
to assess people's reactions to me fairly quickly and I'm usually
right. I read psychology in my last year at Cambridge and this
has helped. Part of that assessment involves putting yourself in
someone else's shoes to see how you might feel if the roles were
reversed, and I'm good at doing that.

Give me an example.

I had to 'board' somebody yesterday who had a psychological
problem. He is a trained pilot — a male, and macho. He's having
to talk things over with a lady doctor and a fairly young one
at that. How is he going to react to me? How does he feel about
his future being decided upon by me? I play on the interview
situation. When he comes in is he tearful, depressed, frightened?
He looks relaxed — I'll be relaxed. If he was depressed, I'd be
motherly. I play on the interaction. I try to respond to people
in a reciprocal way. I've a good sense of humour. You must have
in this job when you've got men in front of you in their
underpants with goodness knows what funny writing on
them.

What makes you angry?

Someone going over my head against a well-founded decision without consulting me. Friends, family, anyone taking me for granted.

I rarely allow myself to be really angry. I feel out of control and it takes too much out of me. I'm outspoken and will tell them directly, 'Please don't do that. I don't like it', but I rarely shout at them.

I'm afraid of heights, but I'll go abseiling. I hate putting my face underwater, so I'll do canoe capsizing drills. I'll have a go and push myself to do it. I'm physically inferior to most men but I don't want to be big and beefy. However, it makes me angry when I'm told, 'You're a woman. You're not physically able to carry a stretcher.' I would like to be asked first whether I would like to try carrying a stretcher to see how I get on.

What are you most proud of?

I'm very proud of working for the Navy. We have manpower and monetary problems in the service but I'm very proud to wear the Navy uniform. I'm proud of what I've achieved; of being the first woman Naval Surgeon Commander. Part of that pride goes to my parents. They put an awful lot into seeing me through grammar school, public school, university, then medical school. My mother saw me a few weeks ago and she can't wait for her friends to come round for tea and to chat about it. My father is extremely proud that I followed in his footsteps and became a doctor.

I'm proud of my sister and brother-in-law and that it was his influence that allowed me to see what the Navy did and to join up. I'm proud that I can still look up to my sister as a barrister, a naval wife and super mother to her little boy. She works, runs the home and leads a very busy social life.

I'm not married. I might have made an appalling wife and a dreadful mother. I don't know, but I'm happy and proud in the niche I've made for myself in my work.

My proudest moment was being promoted to Commander.

Do you have a personal vision?

I would like to see more women doing what I am doing. I do quite a bit of recruiting of female medical officers. I tell them it's a male environment and you must enjoy being with men, ignore the male jokes and childishness and the often prevalent male chauvinist attitude towards women. But if you concentrate on what you want to do, a medical career in the Navy can be an extremely challenging, satisfying and rewarding one, as I have found to my great delight.

Jenny Hilton.

Jenny Hilton

Commander, Metropolitan Police

Predictably, setting up an interview with a member of the Metropolitan Police was not easy. My request to interview Commander Hilton had to be made in triplicate, and six weeks later when I'd still heard nothing, I felt sure the Police National Computer had thrown up something nasty from my past which prevented the interview from going ahead. Finally, the appointment was made and I found myself face-to-face with Commander Hilton in her Kingsbury office. Photography is one of her hobbies and I glanced enviously at massive blow-up photos, panoramic views of exotic places, which adorned the otherwise bare office walls.

You've been in the police force for thirty years. How did you come to join?

I was 18, had failed my A levels, so couldn't go to university. I felt ashamed that the amount of money spent on my education seemed to have been wasted. That motivated me to look for a job that required no further expenditure in terms of a costly training. It was perhaps a curious, limiting way of seeking a career.

It was the time when most women went into teaching, or nursing. I wanted something more challenging, more in the mainstream of life as I saw it. As a child I had fantasies about becoming an explorer or missionary. I always wanted to travel a lot. I was born in Cyprus, and lived in Greece when I was 9 until I was 11. I suppose I was looking for an occupation which was going to be an adventure.

There's a family tradition of amateur social work. I had an aunt in mental welfare — that sort of thing. I thought the police force would combine my desire to help others with my desire for excitement and challenge quite well.

What qualifications did you need to join in those days?

An essay and a few sums. Nowadays it's a bit more rigorous and formal; there are written and aptitude tests. We are looking for the right *personality*, a much harder thing to test. I got in and, because it's a wholly democratic organization, everyone starts off as a constable and works their way up through the ranks. You were promoted to the first two ranks effectively by taking exams. I did five years as a constable. There is an accelerated promotion scheme now, but that wasn't available then.

When I joined there were 450 women in the Met out of a total of 17000; a larger proportion than in other forces in the country. Devon and Cornwall didn't have any women at all until 1948. Nowadays there are 2500 in a complement of 27000 and another 10000 in the rest of the country.

In those days, women officers were allocated to the busier stations. There were a lot in West End Central mainly because of the problems of prostitution among young girls; similarly, a lot in Paddington.

I started off in the East End — much more interesting. I did far more general police duty rather than specializing in the problems of missing girls, neglected children and prostitution, although we had about 100 regular prostitutes because of the large seafaring community! There were 12 female officers and we dealt with the full range of normal problems: drunks, thieves, etc. That was 1956, long before the Equal Opportunities Act which radically changed the role of women in the police force.

At that time, women police officers were the only people actually working in the family. The vast army of statutory social workers that exists today just wasn't there then. We operated through children's officers, Church Army, Salvation Army. In those days children's officers only looked after children in care, in children's homes, due to neglect or the subject of a care order. They were only concerned with the child, not the family as a whole. One of the things the police service did was work with families in their homes, doing much of the visiting present day social workers now undertake. At that time, in many ways, women police officers were the only form of social support for problem families. We had an extra five weeks' training during our first two years because we were specialists in child neglect, abuse and cruelty, often with a caseload of problem families. That aspect of police work has vanished.

At the point when the equal opportunities legislation was implemented (1975) there were still remnants of this role but the effect of the Sex Discrimination Act was to de-value the role of women police officers. They were made to feel their old role was totally unimportant, which of course it was not.

When did you decide to climb the ranks?

I think I was always ambitious. Nowadays it's acceptable for women to be ambitious but it wasn't then; we weren't encouraged to get on in the Force. Many women thought the real job was in the lower ranks on the streets. That's true. It is. Those who enjoy doing that seldom want to become managers and remove themselves from the front line. It's understandable. In some ways it's easier to do a job where you are continuously stimulated by outside events without having to plan or think ahead. You make instant decisions.

Did you think that the switch of emphasis from being active on the frontline to being a manager was suddenly more attractive to you, or was it the only option available — you are either on or off the street?

I didn't think through the consequences of promotion and what it would be like; I just decided to have a go. I was very surprised when I achieved the first couple of ranks. After that, you assume you will be able to manage it the next time.

There's a mixture of duties in all police work. For instance in the recent elections (1987) I found myself back on the streets. I was on duty outside the Tory Party conference, taking instant decisions.

When did your first promotion take place and what was it?

Sergeant. I passed the exams and eventually was posted out to the district covering East Ham, Plaistow, Dagenham, Ilford. There were about 20 women police officers covering the whole of that area so a lot of my time was spent travelling around the area providing back-up to policewomen doing an almost wholly specialist job with children and young people.

It was purely an accident of my posting that I didn't become one of those specialist female police officers. As you get on in the service, the organization increasingly listens to where you would like to go, but basically you go where you are told. I was three and a half years at East Ham, K division.

In those days, women police officers had their own separate hierarchy within the organization. We were a separate force, with our own inspectors and chief superintendents; women used to supervise women. That all changed in 1975 with the equal opportunities legislation, and we became absorbed into the mainstream of the police force, often supervising men directly.

In 1964, I passed the Inspector's exam and went down to the police college in Bramshill, Hampshire for the six month inspector's training course. There were six women out of 70. I enjoyed it enormously because in those days we didn't have television to educate us and in order to facilitate the entrance of police officers with varying backgrounds and standards of education, half the curriculum was academic studies: geography, history, English literature, current affairs, that sort of thing. There's still quite a lot of current affairs and economics in today's syllabus.

In 1965, I became an Inspector at Caledonian Road and went on the directing staff course at the police college the following year. About that time the police scholarship scheme started. Initially it was only offered to bright sergeants on accelerated promotion but by 1966 they were beginning to offer it to Inspectors. I got a Bramshill scholarship as it was called, and went to Manchester University to study psychology for three years. In my fourth year, as a result of a recommendation from our community relations department, I studied race relations, looking at the employment aspirations of black school leavers. It was a very valuable and important time for me. It helped me regain the confidence I lost when I failed my A levels.

I did a year as Inspector at Hammersmith and got promoted to Chief Inspector in the early seventies. I returned to police staff college for a further two years and became the first person to teach psychology there. I missed the initial traumas of women being absorbed into the male structure. It was others who bore the brunt of the first changes, although some of the demoralization of women had begun before I went to police college.

In 1975 I went before the selection board for Superintendents and failed. That was a low time. I don't think people realize or appreciate fully just how traumatizing failure can be. I felt utterly rejected by the organization. I had to deal with the desolation as best I could and get over it somehow and keep going. That experience gave me a valuable insight which now enables me to encourage and support fellow officers facing the same or similar difficulties.

How did the men take to being supervised by women after the changes in the Force due to equal opportunities legislation?

There were no particular difficulties from the men you supervised. I think rank in the force is such an important thing it overrides gender differences. Initially when they were told they were to have a female inspector the first reaction, before meeting you was, 'Gosh, we're having a woman!'

'Gosh!' — enthusiasm?

'Gosh!' — interest, but increasingly it's 'Gosh!' — enthusiasm because most women who achieve high rank are good at their jobs. In the early days it was so unusual to have a woman Inspector, it was almost a cachet.

I became Chief Superintendent at Chiswick and consequently responsible for policing Brentford football club for three and a half years. It was great fun standing on the terraces, organizing a small army of police officers on crowd control, dealing with public order offenders.

I enjoyed it for the first two years but then tired of the standard of football more than anything else — I kept wishing they'd get themselves promoted to the second division!

Have you encountered discouragement or hostility as a woman in the police force?

Well, I'm not your stereotypically quiet woman. I'm outspoken, sometimes critical of the organization, which is seen as boat-rocking, upsetting a comfortable arrangement. People prefer not to look at the deficiencies of a system.

I've learned to be more tactful and to keep my thoughts and aspirations under wraps because I see it as counterproductive. Sometimes, however, it's difficult to resist the urge to nail one's colours to the mast. You have to live with yourself but you have to live and work with others as well. It takes courage to say what you think and over the years I've realized I am brave. I don't mind speaking out but I make sure nowadays it's appropriate. I still have to test my courage occasionally because I get so irritated!

I worry about compromising my principles sometimes. Being opposed to capital punishment, for instance, I usually find myself in the minority of one. Gradually I've found there are others in the force who share my views and that gives me strength and comfort. But almost all political discussions find me in the minority. I'm left of centre whereas most police officers are supposed to be right of centre.

I was slightly ahead of my time in talking about the needs of the community and whether we should be more accountable. Like many professionals such as doctors or lawyers, the police assume they know best. Ten years ago it was uncomfortable to hear someone say that just because the police thought it was right to do something it might not necessarily suit the needs of a particular community. We shouldn't make assumptions that people want us to concentrate resources on capturing big-time criminals when perhaps they really want us to concentrate on detecting rapists, deal with hooligans or people parking cars on pavements illegally. Those differences of concern are often thought of as trivial.

There's a definite need to reform various police systems that serve no purpose at all but are there because they've always been there and that's the way things have always been done. It improved a lot under Sir Kenneth Newman.

I suppose I'm a thorn in the side of the organization, but I think it's a valuable part of my contribution.

When were you promoted to commander?

In 1979. You have to be recommended, put yourself forward and after a series of extended interviews you are selected for the senior command course and go into a national pool of candidates. My rank is equivalent to Assistant Chief Constable. We all go through the same course.

I think my sex was a handicap then. Most officers having

completed the course rapidly get promoted to Commander or Assistant Chief Constable. It took me from 1979 to 1984 to get to the rank of Commander. If there's a gap in my progress, that would be it, although it's difficult to disentangle the precise reason for the delay. Perhaps my particular qualities were not in favour at that time; it wasn't a time for innovators. People with traditional views and attitudes were being promoted, not people like me.

At the beginning of 1983 under Metropolitan Police Commissioner Sir Kenneth Newman, I got swept into one of the planning committees at the Yard. That totally changed my position. It was a very exciting time. It became clear the force was about to change and I began to feel that at last I might have a little influence — which I suppose has always been my ambition, to be in a position of influence, rather than have power over people. The whole of the Yard was being reorganized, along with the force generally. I could be creative, put forward ideas, consult with different people. Of the four major departments at the Yard, I was in charge of planning in the communications, traffic technology department. There were no other women Chief Superintendents in similar posts. I did that for 15 months and was then promoted to Commander.

Working for an Assistant Commissioner, right at the power base of the organization, I had a good opportunity to remind the right people of my ambition and qualities. I was in the right place at the time. No matter how effective you are as a Chief Superintendent there are 200 others in the force and it's difficult to get recognition. Progress in any organization is a matter of letting people know you've the right skills, experience and ability to achieve things. You like to think your talents are exposed on a platter for all to see, but they aren't, they're wrapped up inside us.

As Commander, I continued my organizational work at the Yard and was also in charge of the Obscene Publications Branch, together with the branch that deals with all new projects: neighbourhood policing; a whole range of innovations on the uniform side. It was a very big spread of activities and I enjoyed it tremendously.

Just before Christmas 1986, I was boarded for Deputy Assistant Commissioner, but I failed. I wasn't particularly resentful; no woman has ever reached that rank and the people who were selected are very good.

Queen Elizabeth I. Reproduced courtesy of the National Portrait Gallery.

Will you keep trying?

At this level you don't exactly keep trying, you are 'invited to appear'; so I hope I get invited to appear again very soon! This current job is intended to enhance my career opportunities. I am specifically responsible for personnel, discipline, and community relations for the whole of the north west area of London. I am deputy in command of roughly 2 000 officers and 500 civilian staff.

Who is your hero or heroine?

Going back to my desire to be an explorer and my admiration for those with the ability to survive against all the odds, it would have to be Robinson Crusoe. But as you become older, I think you identify more with your own sex. My heroines are Queen Elizabeth and Mary Kingsley. *Travels in Africa* — that takes me back to explorers, the pioneering spirit, coping in adverse circumstances, people with courage. Mary Wollstonecraft.

What kind of support have you most valued?

On the odd occasions when I want to moan, groan and grumble, the people who are prepared to listen. In the force we are trying increasingly to introduce a more consultative style of management. It's been so rare for officers to have someone to listen to their problems and difficulties, someone to talk things over with them.

Acceptance of my idiosyncracies. Tolerance of my sometimes outlandish views. People who haven't minded when I've spoken my mind and said things that are unpopular.

Have you had to make sacrifices and what do you feel about having made them?

Not consciously. I suppose not being married with children could be seen as a sacrifice. I think of it more in terms of an option I didn't pursue.

I would love to have been involved in politics. Perhaps when I retire I'll take it up. A police officer has to be politically neutral and that's been a difficulty for me. I would have liked to campaign for specific issues, as you can in other jobs.

Mary Kingsley. Reproduced courtesy of the National Portrait Gallery.

What kinds of things do you do to look after yourself?

I go swimming once a week. I'm quite good at giving myself time off. I recently took a diploma in art history. I'm good at being off duty, when I'm off duty. I don't take loads of work home. I may be dedicated to my job but I can switch off quite easily, do something very different. I find that very liberating.

I enjoy foreign travel and amateur photography. Travel satisfies the explorer instinct, though I'm not very athletic and I've no idea how I would have coped had I had to explore the swamps of the Amazon!

What lessons have you learned?

So many. Appreciation of other people's problems. I'm much less self-centred than I used to be. You start out in life thinking you're very much the centre of the universe.

What makes you angry and what makes you laugh?

I get angry with what I think is stupidity, blind emotional stubbornness, bigotry, clinging to traditional values just because it's comfortable, when everything around you dictates change is necessary. It's arrogant of me, I know, and I have to keep myself well under control.

I think I laugh quite a lot at the ridiculous and silly jokes.

Of what are you most proud?

My academic achievements. Although I think we have all been given certain gifts and talents, so we shouldn't really be proud of exploiting innate abilities.

The contribution I've made to changes in the force over the last four years. Here and there I've influenced policy, shifted things a little bit — though it's very hard to be sure because there are so many hands involved in changing the organization and much of it has been a joint effort. But I had a picture of how my department at the Yard would be at the end of two years and it did more or less turn out exactly as I had hoped.

Do you have a personal vision — perhaps in terms of your work?

It's all mixed up with hopes and ambitions. I hope the force becomes much more genuinely accountable than perhaps we are now. I would like us to be more responsive to what the community wants us to do. But I believe anxiety about communicating with those who've an axe to grind, or a particular sectarian viewpoint to express, has lead to a general lack of confidence within the force. The result is we cannot listen and respond clearly to the needs of the community. We often find ourselves trapped between conflicting interests and that's an extremely painful situation to be in. Our lack of confidence means we still tend to say we know best, and make decisions in a vacuum.

It's also painful working through various selfish viewpoints. In the consultative groups that have been set up nationwide, it's not easy to disentangle conflicting wishes of what we should do. We don't have the resources to tackle a task 20 different ways to see which one is right, so we are often forced into making unpopular choices. We do try to be responsive to people's needs,

Mary Wollstonecraft. Reproduced courtesy of the National Portrait Gallery.

but usually end up not being so and that's a very difficult situation to be in and to accept. I think we have moved from saying: 'Yes, we've heard what you have to say, but we know best.' We do have a unique overview of the community, but we've become embedded in all the messages and research information we receive and I think we need to work our way through that into a position where we can communicate quite clearly that we've heard all the messages and do understand people's problems. However, it has to be a two-way communication process. The public has got to be confident that we have heard and understood their concerns and difficulties, but, because of a more serious problem elsewhere, we're not able to do exactly as they want. They need to understand why we have had to take a certain unpopular decision which sometimes appears so arbitrary. I don't think we've been sufficiently clear why we make certain decisions. We're trying very hard with the consultative groups, not only talking to councillors, but community leaders and many other interested parties, and a dialogue is taking place.

I hope, as we begin to understand each other's viewpoint and know more about each other's organizations, cultures and what the specific problems are, we can move into a position where we can communicate clearly and freely to each other. I don't think we can do it unless both sides have a common range and pool of information. The police force has a lot of it, others have some too and it needs to be brought together in a more coherent manner and then we can have informed discussion about what is to be done.

Rabbi Julia Neuberger.

Julia Neuberger

Rabbi

*I've no idea where Julia finds the time to do everything she does.
I was allocated 45 minutes in between her breakfast and one of
her regular LBC Radio contributions. Her abundant energy made
me feel like a clapped out old crock firing on three cylinders
instead of six!*

Is it difficult for women to become rabbis?

It was but it isn't anymore. This year, the first-year class at Leo
Baeck College where I teach is entirely female. It's the first time
that's happened. It's not amazingly significant but it's interesting.
You'll soon have Jewish women going into the rabbinate and no
men. You could say all sorts of things about the rabbinate being
badly paid, and women going for badly paid jobs. It's true. I think
it's interesting that as some of the less well paid jobs have opened
up to women, many of them have gone into those jobs and
pressure to pay more has been taken off. Nursing is an interesting
example of where men have gone in and the pressure for higher
pay has come on. I think there is a very signficant correlation
between the number of women in higher positions in the
professions and the degree of campaigning for higher pay.

When did you decide to become a rabbi?

I wanted to be an archaeologist. It still feels accidental. I was doing
Babylonian archaeology at Cambridge. I knew what I wanted to
do. I didn't want to dig; I wanted to be on site identifying finds.
But it was impossible to go anywhere as a British Jew.

My minority subject at university was Hebrew, which I'd taken
as a soft option because I already knew some. As a result of the
refusals I changed my course and did Hebrew as my main subject
and Assyriology as the second subject and became very interested
in mediaeval Judeo-Christian relationships. But the weird thing
about it was, I had no idea what I would do after that. Something
vaguely academic I supposed. One of the people teaching me
was Nicholas de Lange, who's been a considerable influence in
my life. He suggested I should become a rabbi. Later on he became
one himself.

I can remember it clearly. He took me out to supper one evening
after an incredibly long tutorial. He sat at the opposite side of
the table and said 'Look, I think you ought to become a rabbi.'
I squawked with rage and poured soup down my front.

In my fourth year he arranged for me to go down to London
one day a week to rabbinic college to see whether I would like
it. It's really as a result of that that I took the decision.

I'm lousy in libraries. I get very cheesed off sitting there for
long periods of time, so a straight academic Ph.D. type of life
would drive me up the wall! It wasn't something I did out of rage
at being rejected as an archaeologist, because I could have done
that in Israel if I'd wanted to. Nicholas made it possible to examine
it as an option, and it seemed a very good option although it wasn't
how I perceived my life, and it still isn't!

What does being a rabbi entail?

Basic things like taking services.

Like an Anglican vicar?

Not really, it involves more teaching. A rabbi is much less spiritual,
in that Judaism has no sacrament and therefore, although we
conduct or lead services, anyone else could do the same. There's
quite a lot of pastoral work and endless committee meetings. It
is geared towards teaching and away from sacraments. Compared
to Christianity we are not separate. We are not priests, we are
teachers. Rabbi means teacher. I teach kids religion in schools
and Hebrew in adult education.

Tonight we'll have a seminar instead of a proper service, to
discuss Jewish attitudes towards abortion because of the Alton
private member's parliamentary Bill promoting a reduction in the

number of weeks in which an abortion may be carried out legally. Tomorrow I won't give a sermon, I'll read a portion from the Law and then explain it. I conduct a fair number of quite didactic-style sermons.

Who has inspired you over the years?

Vicky Clement-Jones, the founder of an organization called BACUP, the British Association of Cancer United Patients. This is an information service for cancer sufferers. It's very medical, with experienced nurses on its telephone counselling service. It also publishes books to help people learn to live with cancer. Vicky was a very young, brilliant doctor, a cancer specialist found to have ovarian cancer. She used the awful events in her life to be helpful to others and having battled with it in the most amazing way, she died last summer (1987). She wasn't at all pious or worthy — there was nothing sweet about her. She was a very strong, impressive character and one of the most inspiring people I've ever met.

Vicky was very good at drawing public attention to the plight of cancer sufferers. She was a role model, in that I would very much like to continue her important work, because I'm involved in hospices, caring for the dying and terminally sick, and I don't think there's nearly enough positive information available to cancer patients.

Another inspiring person is Rabbi Hugo Gryn, now in his mid-fifties but who I first knew as a child. When I was a student and before I became a Rabbi, I never really appreciated the true quality of the work he was doing, but as I get older he influences me enormously. He's very much a pastoral rabbi, very interested in how relationships between organizations work — whether you can actually have an organization that provides help to people, or whether it becomes a political entity on its own and doesn't provide the service it's supposed to provide. It's something that always interests me, particularly in the voluntary sector. Voluntary organizations have this awful history of internecine warfare and I wonder just how much of the service they are supposed to provide they actually do provide. Rabbi Gryn is very good at straightening out organizations caught in that kind of trap and helping them clarify and deal with their own distress so that they can help the people they are supposed to be helping. It's a skill I admire very much and I've tried to learn from that.

Vicky Clement-Jones. Photograph by David Bocking.

Rabbi Hugo Gryn.

I hugely admire Louis Blom-Cooper, a barrister, who chaired the Jasmine Beckford child abuse inquiry, and he's currently chairing another one. He seems to have fought for all the right causes. I don't regard him as a role model exactly, but I do admire him tremendously.

Anthony Kenny, who was the Master of Balliol, I admire very much. He's the most honest person I've ever met. He was a priest and wrote a book about his leaving the Catholic Church, called *The Path From Rome*. We overlapped a bit in that I was a student rabbi in Liverpool a long time ago and he was a young priest there at the same time. He is painfully honest and, because of that, life is often difficult for him.

I'm very moved by the writing of a friend of mine, Angela Levin, a journalist who sees into individuals in a quite extraordinary way.

I respect Anthony Lester, a human rights lawyer, who was involved in the Spycatcher case. He's what I call a 'hot lawyer', rather than a cold one. He takes on cases he minds about. I'm always interested in people who campaign *within* the legal system, because in the end I think that's the only way you actually get anywhere. He's done a lot of work on equality legislation. He's been a feminist in the kind of way I admire very much.

I'm very drawn to Mother Frances Domenica. She runs the Helen House Children's Hospice in Oxford. A very, very impressive woman for a variety of reasons, quite apart from her religious work. She's absolutely not a role model as she has almost no fear of death, to the extent of feeling that it's legitimate not to worry about one's body at all. That's so different from any Jewish perspective, and I find all of that very foreign, but I think her work is stunning and sensational. I believe she has huge inner strength.

Dr Sheila Cassidy is a good example of inner strength, too. She runs St Luke's Hospice in Plymouth. I don't share many of her views but I very much respect the work that she does.

Because of their particular religious beliefs and the fact they have chosen to enter a convent life they could in no way be role models, but it's the remarkable work they do and their incredible inner strength that I so admire, and it inspires me.

What's the difference in the Jewish attitude towards the body?

It's a life-preserving, self-preserving attitude. You do have responsibilities to look after yourself physically. You can't destroy yourself. Suicide is wholly wrong, but so, in a sense, is martyrdom. Judaism doesn't have the admiration of martyrdom that Christianity does, although there are Jewish martyrs. It's a different approach. There's less certainty about the after-life; there isn't the body denial thing in Judaism. You can see this in our attitude to sex. In Judaism sex is regarded as, on the whole, good; in Christianity it's a sin, something to be pushed away.

Have you set yourself specific goals and have they changed?

Constantly, and they always change. One that has remained the same is my ambition to write a really serious book. I have written serious books like the one for nurses on the care of the dying, of which I'm extremely proud. But it's not very long or weighty and I want to write 'a great work'. I hope to do it soon. I'm particularly interested in the issue of collaboration and in why good people collaborate with evil regimes, bad people with bad regimes, whether people are morally neutral. I'm interested in how all that works.

Is being a woman an intrinsic part of what you do?

Yes. I am sure it affects enormously the things I get involved in. Being a rabbi means you can get involved in absolutely everything and anything. It's one of those jobs where you make a list and the list gets longer and never shorter.

I work with nurses and in the hospice area where there are many women working. On the whole I think I have a more female attitude to bereavement counselling. I often work more with widows than widowers.

What do you bring to your job as a woman?

I don't know. You can't tell. I don't know what I'd have brought to the job had I been male. It's almost impossible to judge that.

No special qualities?

No, because I might have had them as a man — far less likely — but some would say because I'm so high-profile I have rather more male qualities than most women, so I'm not sure I can assess that. To the extent that I'm interested in women's issues, yes, but beyond that I'm not sure about my individual qualities.

What kind of professional and family support do you have and value?

Masses of family support and an extremely supportive husband. He's had to put up with rather a lot, because I do tend to be out at the most extraordinary times and it does mean, particularly since we have children — Harriet's eight and Matthew's six — he can be landed with some complicated business of taking a child out to X because I'm just not around. My job's on-call, his isn't. He has done an enormous amount of picking up pieces, domestically, where I haven't been able to. What I mean is, I think he does more than 50 per cent of that and therefore it's hugely supportive. 50-50 seems fair. More than 50 per cent is a bonus.

Women friends seem to be more supportive than men.

How do you deal with cricitism, public and private?

Oh, the two fingers in the air attitude to life! No analysis or anything like that. I think if you're in the sort of position I'm in, you are bound to get criticized. Some of it will be well-founded and some of it won't. I believe an awful lot of criticism is an expression of jealousy, particularly within the Jewish community. Within my local community they are smashing. I've had a few comments that have shaken me a bit, regarding my high public profile. But what can I do? I know who my friends are. Serious criticism tends to come from my friends, but it doesn't manifest itself as direct criticism. It's more an expression of an opinion in a discussion and I do take that very seriously.

Have you had to compromise yourself in any way because you're a woman?

I suspect not. I suspect I've had considerable advantages being a woman. The freak value of being one of the early woman rabbis means I've not had to compromise particularly. I've had to compromise doing television work. It makes me furious having my hair gummed together with sticky substances and being covered in make-up, which gives me spots. I hate and loathe all of that. It's only recently, as I've become more senior and certain of my own ground, that I can say to the TV company, 'Sorry, but I'm not having that awful muck on my face.' It's left me with an abiding skin allergy which is a real drag.

But you've not compromised your principles?

I don't think so. Maybe I have. That would be even worse wouldn't it? I'm not very compromising on the whole, but I'm always willing to apologize. Men tend not to do that. I think saying sorry is a terribly easy thing to do, it often makes people feel 300 million times better and what has it cost you? That way you never have to compromise, you can carry on along the same track, but you can say you're sorry. You don't want to hurt people, or their feelings, but you can be quite firm about how you want to proceed on a particular issue. Quite often apologizing to people makes them realize you didn't mean to hurt them and it makes them change. Men do less of it; women are quite good at it.

Do you find it difficult to put yourself first?

No, not at all.

How do you have fun, relax, enjoy yourself?

I have fun sporadically, in that we go away during school holidays. We have a house in the west of Ireland and I ride and potter around there, cooking, chatting, drinking wine and having very good times with friends. That's a very important bolt hole. I occasionally go for a week on my own during school term so that I can write. That's great!

Seeing friends who are nothing to do with work is very important. It's very hard leading my kind of life to have very much of a social life in London, but I make a big effort to keep it going because I feel very strongly about it.

Going to the movies in the afternoon is one of my big self-indulgences — on my own with a big box of hankies. I go through a cathartic experience and then feel a lot better!

Have you had to make sacrifices and how do you feel about making them?

One of the things about being a rabbi is you don't have weekends and as the children get older you see less of them at the one time when they're at home. I regret and resent that and it's a very major sacrifice for me. I don't enjoy very small children, but I do enjoy them at this age because you can go off and do things with them. That's why I've taken half-term week off, so we can go on expeditions together.

Being a rabbi puts huge strains on your family. They're supposed to do all the good Jewish things like going to synagogue all the time, which is the model you are trying to portray, but on the other hand you have no right to inflict that on your family. It must be up to them as individuals whether or not they come along. It makes for quite a bit of tension, but I would never force my family to do anything. It must be up to them. I can set them examples but I think it's wrong to impose things on your family.

What have been your highest and lowest public and private moments?

My lowest private moment, was, I suppose, public as well: Harriet's illness when she was one year old. She had a kidney disorder and it was very hard to do anything very much. That was clearly the lowest and it went on sporadically until she was three, when she went into remission.

Like most human beings, I find uncertainty hardest to cope with. If you know how awful it is, you can handle it, come to terms with it. But for us there was nothing to come to terms with. We had no idea whether she would survive. It was all pretty terrible.

My husband and I reacted differently. He never wanted to talk about it at all and I wanted to talk about it all the time. Lyndscy, our nanny, who's been with us since Harriet's birth, equally found it very hard. Effectively Harriet had three parents at that point and it was an enormous strain. We coped in a variety of ways. People were very kind and supportive.

The congregation were wonderful, whether it was expressed in people bringing round gefilte fish, or just by being quietly comforting. We had very little of the thing which is actually intolerable — people constantly phoning to say 'How is she?'

The last thing you want to say for the eighth time that day is, 'I don't know.' That's very unsupportive. Although everyone thinks it is, it's not. Gefilte fish, people cooking you a meal, is supportive.

Harriet's illness went on for so long and I can never completely relax about it even now. I can't really believe she'll be OK, because there may be side-effects of the drugs. That causes most of the tension in my life.

I can't think of what *the* highest moment was. But one of them was making a TV programme that I thought was really worth making. I only feel that unequivocally about one, one that I made with Vicky Clement-Jones, a year before she died. She was on a panel of four, discussing with other deeply disabled people in the audience about how human beings face their mortality; talking completely honestly, frankly and unemotionally about how she faced her impending death. I found it very moving and I felt that for once we were making a TV programme that was useful to a lot of people. It's certainly been used endlessly as a teaching aid since. It's the one piece of work where I actually feel we did something wholly right. It didn't seem to me to have a lot of the glitz that TV always has, and which I hate. Nor did it seem to have the faults of most discussion programmes. You don't continue the debate because you're not really debating, you are trying to analyse people's feelings. It was a kind of studio documentary and I'm very proud of it.

Other high moments were getting my degree and becoming a rabbi.

There are frequent odd highs like being asked to be a trustee on the board of something. That's a very great honour. I was terribly honoured to be asked to be on the Ethics Committee of the Royal College of Nursing, and the Council of St George's Medical School. As a non-doctor I think it's very gratifying. I'm invited because I have a particular interest, or because I can be useful to an organization in some way. Increasingly, professional bodies think it's a good idea to have lay people involved, playing a part.

Being asked to write an opinion feature for the *Observer* which I did and enjoyed. It was on secrecy in Britain. Being able to follow through on things. I've done a lot of work on anti-discrimination, a Bill of Rights. Writing articles on issues that I care about passionately, for people to take seriously. Those things give me a high.

Do you find difficulty in separating your public and private lives?

As far as the public is concerned, I've had a reasonably trouble-free run. I think you have to protect your family. People who know me professionally tend to know quite a lot about me privately. Our social and private lives are partly professional because people I meet through work often become very close personal friends. It does mesh in to a considerable extent. But I think in the sense of becoming a rabbi, doing television, writing articles, I've had a relatively easy run. Sometimes it's been more difficult than others, for instance, Harriet's illness, but it's not been very tough very often.

It may be because you are good at what you do and how you handle it.

That may be so, but that often engenders jealousy. People think it obviously isn't difficult for me.

When do you feel most vulnerable?

When I'm tired. When I don't know what I'm talking about. So much of my public life is about confidence and I'm much less confident when I'm tired. Exhaustion leads to vulnerability. I'm very aware of getting older and not having the energy I had at 25.

I cope by doing a bunk! I go to Ireland. I think it's a pity that very, very few people are prepared to do that. If you don't, you have a nervous breakdown or produce very bad work. Ireland has been a wonderful retreat. I can sit at the kitchen table and write half a book and not feel remotely exhausted. It's the air, and the fact that the Irish believe you must never interrupt someone who's being creative. Although they drop in any other moment, they leave me alone if I'm working.

When are you most happy?

I'm happy with lots of friends or when I feel I've done a really good piece of work. Giving a good sermon, running a set of excellent High Holy Days — it doesn't matter what it is — something I've really put my all into.

. . . and angry? How do you deal with it?

I get angry at British snobbery and the constant, constant anti-women remarks people don't know they are making. I never know whether I should pick them up *every* time. I usually do and then I'm labelled a harridan — but two fingers to that! Recently I was at a seminar about arms control. We were discussing flexibility. Some man said, 'Flexibility is what your wife means when she says, "Let's be flexible about that," when she really means, "You do what I say!"' I commented, 'Firstly, that isn't an accurate reflection of most marriages, but secondly, that's very offensive to women.' That kind of anger is assuaged by dealing with it then and there.

The other kind of anger, for example, at the state of our prisons — something people don't mind about hugely — that's much harder to assuage. You try to take action to improve the situation. That's the only way I know of dealing with anger. I don't believe in the 'going-away-to-cool-off' theory of life, because often when you return it's exactly the same, so it's a completely pointless tactic.

I don't get really angry very often. When I do I go white, cold and silent, and am fairly pointed in what I say. I'm a very verbal person and almost always deal with my anger verbally.

What makes you sad?

The hopelessness of trying to do something about the all-pervasive bad attitudes in our society, for example, that it's really OK to get rich at the expense of the poor.

I find public squalor very saddening.

AIDS. All these completely unnecessary, pointless sufferings where the therapy given to try and stop it is so revolting itself.

The needless death of the very young — seven- and ten-year-olds dying of leukemia; young people in their 20s dying through drug abuse. It's not only death of the young in war, because I think there is some meaning in war, but I don't think there is any meaning at all in death from leukemia. The suffering that saddens me about war is the suffering of people who weren't in any sense involved. Not only mothers and wives, but the people whose land is trampled across and the culprit never seen again — what's referred to officially as 'the accident of war'. It saddens me because it is completely irresponsible.

I'm both saddened and angered by what I see as a vast increase in racial prejudice in Britain and the open acceptability of racism.

Do you have a sense of your own spirituality?

Yes, although I think it's a very unconventional one. It's much more related to working with people at times of extraordinary loss, when people are dying or have just been bereaved, than with any kind of sense of the spirit achieved sitting in a synagogue or cathedral. It comes as a result of being together with people at their most profound moments.

How would you like things to be? Do you have a personal vision?

I would like to see a society which is community-based, in which the group recognizes its responsibility to individuals, but in which individuals also recognize their responsibility to the group. Society as a whole doesn't recognize its responsibility to individuals. To talk about freedom is to talk about certain people who have the freedom to do certain things.

I would like to see a completely different philosophy pervading our society and I've no idea how we could achieve that. I have some dim political ideas; I do think that the setting out of a constitution in which we are all clear which responsibilites are whose, would help enormously.

I think our society is about as nasty as I remember it in my 37 years. Most of its values are up the creek and I find it very, very offensive, so my vision would be of trying to change that. Personal wealth is less important than public well-being, which may be to do with public wealth. Public squalor is in itself very degrading; it's not legitimate to allow a greater gap between the rich and the poor.

The only way you can run a society that feels fair is to say that individuals with whom you disagree have a right to express their views. For me that may mean that people whose political views I condemn out of hand must nevertheless have a right to express them. I think that's one of the things we've been wrong about: trying to run extreme right wing groups underground. I suspect you neutralize them better by allowing them to be public.

I would like to see a much less secret society, more open, much more geared towards the common good. How you teach people these are goals worth achieving I don't know, but I try by taking on issue after issue. But it's much more difficult than that, because all you're doing is scratching the surface. Education may achieve it.

The thing I find most depressing at the moment is how materialistic most of the students and young people I meet are. It's coloured the next generation so completely. People see the value of their future in terms of whether or not they'll have a Sony Walkman. It's just horrendous. It means re-educating two generations, minimum, and I find that very depressing.

What lessons have you learned?

That you can't achieve peace quickly is one; that it is worth ploughing on at individual issues; that although it may only scratch the surface and you may only help one or two people in your life, it must be better than helping no-one. You don't have the right to give up, nor have you the right to say, 'I've done enough,' because although you get exhausted and go away for a bit, if you really mind about things you have to come back and fight. You make the same point again and again. People might think, 'What! Her again! How boring!' but you've no option; you've got to carry on fighting.

I've learned that prejudice against women is even deeper than I realized as a child in my equal opportunity family and my single sex school, and that it pervades our society, but that it is not as extreme as the feelings against black or brown people.

I've learned that I no longer believe in rainbow coalitions, because they don't work.

I've learned that single-issue campaigning is better than broad campaigning.

I've learned that being a mother isn't as bad as I thought at first!

I've learned to love the countryside and country pursuits, particularly riding, a slower way of life and, good heavens, gardening!

Bridget Riley.

Bridget Riley CBE

Painter

*Bridget Riley is one of Britain's foremost contemporary painters.
I persuaded her my shorthand could replace the loathesome tape
recorder, but took a friend along to ask the questions so that I
could concentrate properly on my note-taking. The three of us
sat sipping coffee round a large white table, with Bridget Riley
framed in a high-backed, white winged leather chair. The walls
of the part-studio, part-sitting-room were almost completely
hidden behind two huge, vibrantly colourful Riley works of art.
A little over an hour later my companion and I emerged knowing
we'd been given a lot more than just an interview.*

I don't think I ever think of myself as a *woman* painter. It has
never been in my mind that I am different from other painters.
It is in the mind of people who deal with my work. Some do
see it as being very 'feminine' — whatever that may mean — but
I don't think it has ever been an issue for me. I remember Nigel
Gosling, art critic of the *Observer*, reviewing an exhibition of
mine some years ago at The Hayward Gallery, London. He said,
'If I had to track down a feminine footprint here, I would point
to a certain unforced patience, that quality which can add the
thousandth stitch to the nine-hundred-and-ninety-ninth without
a tremor of triumph.' I thought that was a surprising little tribute.

Who has inspired you?

My mother certainly. She had an enormous influence on me. It's
difficult to know how best to convey a sense of her, but people
just loved being with her. She was always able to give a sense

of pleasure to any kind of occasion or event. She was loyal, strong, loving and yet totally flexible in her outlook, often changing her priorities. There was never any sentimental hanging on to previous positions; she was always fresh-minded, always amusing. My friends became her friends and when she died one of these friends said she had a radiance which was a warmth and comfort to everybody. She was a gift simply being alive. It was an enormous stroke of luck to have someone like that as one's mother.

What did you learn from her?

During the war my father was a prisoner of war on the Siamese railway. In three years we had only three postcards from him. We had very little money; we lived in a cottage in Cornwall that was a paradise for children but must have been a nightmare for my mother. There were few amenities: no bath; we got water from a brook; the roof leaked; we had tarpaulins over our beds. It should have been a miserable time, but it wasn't. We had frightfully nice times there. There were certainly fears. My father worried that my mother was untrained. If he did not come back, how would she have kept us? How would we have lived?

My mother took us for walks on the cliffs. She was always pointing out colours: in the sea; the sparkle of dew; changes of colour when the dew was brushed away. If she arranged anything on the table like a bowl of fruit (we only saw two bananas in the village the whole time we were there!) she would point out the different colours. 'Look, it's almost got a blue on it.' She wasn't a painter, she was a 'looker'. The pleasure one could get from looking was part of her personality.

She was very well read. She would read to us at night. When I was 10 or 11 we would have a hip bath in the winter once a week, in front of the fire. At other times we'd top and tail. She would read something from the classics, we would say our prayers together and go to bed. That gave me a taste for reading. As soon as I could I bought a torch and continued to read under the bedclothes.

I lived there for the five years of the war and left in my early teens to go back to our own house in Boston, Lincolnshire.

When did you think you might become a painter?

I always wanted to paint. I had an aunt who spent the war with us. She had been an artist but did not paint or draw anymore.

I always thought that rather strange. I drew the way that all children do. I loved it. It didn't occur to me for a long time what being an artist really involved. I pushed that idea away. Drawing and painting was another matter; I didn't think that meant being an artist. I didn't really face the full implications of my decision to become a painter until I left my first art school, at the age of 21. We had left Cornwall, my father had returned and we were faced with the emotional trauma of adjusting to a total stranger. I had been my mother's companion and had had most of her attention. I became withdrawn and immersed myself in drawing and painting. I was sent home from school for a term for being over-excitable.

My father thought my education had gone to pot. It was true; it had been completely interrupted by the war. He decided that I was quite illiterate and should go to a better school.

I went to a splendidly academic school with my younger sister — Cheltenham Ladies' College. The headmistress was a great support to the children of prisoners of war but was disconcerted and flummoxed when she realized she would have to put me in the bottom class academically. I should have been half-way up the school in terms of my age. I told her not to worry, I would work out my own timetable. She was very relieved and let me go ahead. I came up with art in the morning, art in the afternoon: art on Monday morning, art on Tuesday afternoon, art on Wednesday morning and art on Thursday afternoon!

They had a wonderful art wing. I had never seen such a palace. I was allowed to study art most of the time, but there was also a particularly good course called citizenship. This involved reading newspapers, visiting prisons (but not in the lady bountiful manner), factories, law courts and included a great many other things. It was supposed to be a one-year course but because that was the only thing I could do I repeated it for three!

My parents were desperately worried when I wanted to leave and go to art school. They were both educated and didn't believe in opposing their children's ambitions. They were worried for very different reasons. My father felt it was unlikely I would meet the right sort of person to keep me happy. Mother, more accurately, felt it would be a tremendously hard and lonely life. They both felt that it could lead to unhappiness. They didn't gainsay me, but were worried. It was agreed I could do commercial art because in that way I might make a living.

I met a marvellous teacher who taught me drawing, at

Goldsmith's School of Art. His name was Sam Rabin. In those days you were taught drawing. I was there when class began and ended. For three years I drew day and night. Without realizing it I absorbed, through the techniques of life drawing, many important things such as pictorial organization, structure and the stripping away of the visual image to see what's beneath. For example, when I first drew somebody, Sam Rabin would come up to me and say, 'What's the model doing, sitting or standing? Is your drawing standing?' He taught me to order my work, to develop it in methodical stages, to see a thing as a whole, not in part. He stressed the importance of the relationships between things; how everything matters; what to accept of yourself; how to make an advance and consolidate it; make another advance; not to expect advance after advance; how to raise the level of work achieved slowly; to look at the whole movement of what you are doing. That was gold — and something I have kept with me.

Sam Rabin was a key person. He used to take me to the print and drawing room in the British Museum where you can study and hold in your hands masterpieces by artists like Rembrandt, Raphael and Ingres. He taught me for three years.

Then I went to the Royal College of Art. I wanted to find someone else like that, but there was no-one. I floundered there, and in a way I knew I would, because I had come up against a young artist's worst problem — what to paint and how to paint it. You live every day with the gravity of the problem, surrounded with that experience of uncertainty.

The example of Cezanne makes it plain that you must be workmanlike in what you do. You can't simply go for being an artist as such. You must wait to find something which excites you, fires your imagination, your desire, creates a real longing to do that one thing. If you can centre on that you can make a beginning. You don't worry where you are going because you are moving. Desire is the key. It comes and goes. It's rhythmic. You languish; when you have a problem you become bored. Boredom is a tremendous indicator. Your energy goes; it caves in on you; you can't do anything. That's very frightening but you must listen because you are being told that whatever it is you are doing it is not quite right. It may only need a small adjustment or it may need more drastic treatment.

There are a bewildering number of directions you can go, but if it's not right it doesn't *feel* right. You are much further forward even if it takes you all morning to make the decision not to do something because it doesn't feel right. That's true for me, at least.

Having no formal academic education has been a great asset. Many artists realize you cannot do what has been done before. You must do something that meets your own criteria and you have to form those criteria. Being an artist is a great responsibility and can be very confusing. I often find my way in daydreams and then I start to work. You have a gigantic freedom as you are re-awakened. It never occurred to me I could earn my living as an artist. It never occurred to me that I would be anything other than a figurative painter, painting people, external reality and what you can actually see around you.

I began to meet people, to travel, to understand what happened in art from the nineteenth century onwards; what amazing things had been done and how much has been achieved. This is something you find out after art school. I became deeply interested; I got fired. I didn't know what form it was going to take.

I was 28 years old at this time. I was having an extremely immature affair with a very nice man who was older than me. I was difficult and hard to handle, doing things he just couldn't be bothered with. He decided to end the affair. I was angry and hurt. I thought. 'I'm not going to discuss anything with you. I can't communicate verbally with you, so what's the point in trying? But I'll paint you a message so loud and clear you'll know exactly how I feel.' It was then that I started my black and whites.

When I gave up painting external reality I realized I was giving up a vast pleasure and that from now on it was not going to be pleasurable. No more following a form with the pencil; that would go. It would be a sacrifice — but you go on making sacrifices. I could have stayed painting black and white paintings but I eroded them by introducing greys, the things that lay between. I felt myself erode them. I knew that I was destroying a previous position. You can't go on holding an extreme position. To do so would mean turning it into the very opposite.

Do you feel lonely or alone at times?

Yes, I do. Being a painter is lonely. My life is not at all exciting now, although at one time it was the reverse and I found it was bad for my work. Most painters find this is so. You can see from other artists' lives that those who take the risks in their personal lives seldom take them in their work and that those who have taken the risks in their work have had very secure personal lives. It seems to be one or the other, not both. If your work is going well you are comforted, nourished and protected by it. It's difficult when it's going badly.

Does other people's criticism matter?

Less and less, but I can still be very hurt that someone misses the point or misunderstands my work, because I want people to enjoy my paintings, I want to give them the freedom and elation. I want them to feel as I do, or can sometimes, and to have this particular joy.

I do a certain amount of lecturing. My aim is to make people feel alive. If there are good questions at the end of a lecture that gives me a feeling of pleasure and excitement.

Of what are you most proud? Yourself?

I don't feel proud of myself. That's the truth. I feel excited, and proud, when I can fire people — it's like hearing a beautiful piece of music.

And what about failure?

We all fail. Failure is inevitable but the degree of it is what's important. When I don't know what my work is saying, I say so. It's important to say so if you don't know. Then people will tell me what they think I was or am doing. I get the most amazing insights that way. Sometimes they can see something more clearly in the image, even if I don't know exactly what it is myself. I'm greatly encouraged when people come and tell me what they see. Seeing is a very serious matter. Trying to be an artist is a big responsibility. It is the most serious thing there is.

What do you do for yourself?

Now I have people I can talk to. That's very valuable, but I seldom talk about things that really matter. You cannot take away the energy, it's a very internal thing. All artists have part of themselves that they can never share with anyone else.

How do you nourish yourself?

Nature and the museums. I go to Cornwall; I have a garden; I have a little house in France with a big studio and a lot of privacy. I look at paintings. In the spring I went to Paris with a friend with whom I can *really* talk. He lives abroad, but we talk on the phone — we're together that way. He loves paintings as much as I do and we had a real binge: the Louvre, a Matisse exhibition, the Musée d'Orsay; St Chapelle, and the Lion and Unicorn tapestry in the Cluny Museum. That's my food. Listening to music, most of all Mozart, reading slowly and carefully — I love Proust — and getting a little drunk now and then!

Is it difficult keeping the public and private lives separate?

I have had to learn how to cope. You learn that people will help. When you start off, people come forward to help you. There are roles to play, especially at openings, which are an ordeal for all artists. The sympathy is there for you, very kindly, although no-one really listens to what you say on those sorts of occasions. But there's someone to get you through it somehow if you let them, someone who will hold your glass for you!

What lessons have you learned?

Other artists teach you. There is one thing I would like to say to young artists and it is this: look at the great painters; don't be frightened of them, they've seen more clearly, experienced more deeply and are more explicit. Weaker artists are confused. Read the best, look at the best. Don't look at your contemporaries, look back at the past.

Delacroix has been an example in many ways but mostly in the spirit which runs through his journals. Best of all you work with love and desire, next you work with will, and finally, if all else fails, you work with bloody obstinacy!

Mikki Doyle taken after a riot at which rock-throwing anti-Paul Robeson demonstrators stormed a peaceful Labor Day open air concert at Peekesville, New York, 4th September, 1949, where he made a guest appearance.

Mikki Doyle

Communist Party member

They don't make people like Mikki Doyle anymore. Born in America a year before the Bolshevik revolution, she survived the McCarthy era in the US and was deported to England with her Scottish husband in the mid-fifties. In her 70s, recently widowed, and plagued by ill-health, Mikki is forced to take a back seat on the barricades, but from the way the phone rang itself off the hook during our conversation, it's obvious she'll continue campaigning against racism and for women's right until she drops.

Why are you such a committed campaigner against racism?

In the beginning, I realize now, I lived in and never went outside a working class white ghetto. I was eight years old before I saw a black person. It was 1924; my father brought home a paper showing a handsome black man running as a candidate for the New York State legislature, representing the Socialist Party.

I remember the page even now; it was full of all these white men (no women of course, they weren't *that* aware!) and this one black man. I said to my father, 'What's the matter with this picture?' He explained the man's skin was black, and suddenly I was aware of another people, another culture. We underestimate the influences on children's minds — it stuck with me.

I don't know exactly what made me respond the way I did but I felt deeply about the way black people were treated. In those days in the States it was called the Negro question. I had a great sensitivity to their suffering and the racial discrimination made me very angry.

Later on, in my 20s, married with two kids, I began to become more politically aware. I was beginning to read newspapers. I read the *Daily Worker*; I couldn't understand the sectarian political jargon, but there was an article very simply written that blew my mind.

It was the 1930s, there were lynchings in the Southern States, the Ku Klux Klan (that is still going on today, of course). Anyway, the Socialist Party attacked both white racism and black racism. The Communist Party wrote a paper attacking the Socialist Party, saying there's no such thing as black racism in a white dominated society.

Today we have black power in Africa, Zimbabwe, etc., but if you're white and on the receiving end, you can't accuse black people of racism because they don't have the power to crack the white racism. They may be anti-white, but it's called black nationalism.

Why did you combine your non-racist awareness with communism?

From its inception, the United States Communist Party was way ahead of all organizations, including the few black organizations that existed in the States, in that it always made the struggle against racism a central part of its programme.

The first year the Party ran in the US Presidential elections, we had William Z. Foster and James Ford (a black), the originators of what we call today the black civil rights movement. The US Communist Party was the forerunner of all that.

The Party had all the great black intellectuals writing articles about the slave struggle: Frederick Douglass the great black abolishionist, W.E.B. Dubois — he wasn't a member of the Communist Party but he was very close to us and we published his writings. We had all kinds of leading educated blacks like Doxie Wilkinson — I knew them all!

It was through the US Communist Party that I learned the first person to give his life as a soldier in the American Revolutionary War was Crispus Attucks, a black man. We were never taught that in school. Black history is more commonly taught nowadays, though still not enough.

If you wanted to stay in the Party you had to get rid of any racism you might feel. Otherwise you were put through a kangaroo court, told to get rid of it fast, and if you couldn't, you were expelled. To me this was so logical; it opened up a new world to me. It altered my life.

How did you go about ridding yourself of your own racism?

Discussions. And I read everything the Party published. I learned very quickly. I became very sensitive to black issues, and eventually, around 1938 or 1939, I was sent into Harlem to raise funds to build the first hospital there. It was a such a break. They were the richest and most rewarding years of my life. I learned about a new culture, I studied all about slavery, and conducted classes on the fundamentals of Marxism to black people in Harlem schools and in Bedford Stuyvessant, the largest black area in North America.

At that time, to rationalize the obscenity of slavery, there evolved a whole pseudo science, pseudo psychology, pseudo philosophy about the existence of an inferior race. To combat this I talked about slavery and explained there had been white slaves from England. No-one knew about that — you weren't taught that, probably not even now. Black people certainly didn't know. White people were called 'indentured slaves'; if you stole two shillings in Britain off you went to the colonies. Although the whites could never pay off their debt, they could escape and be assimilated in the States. If you were black and escaped to the North, it wasn't so easy!

At first I had to win my spurs; black people weren't prepared to accept little old whitey! But because I was unsure of myself, modest, and sensitive to their plight, I won their trust. So much so, I remember I was in a car full of black men and women and they forgot I was white. They were talking about some black comrade who was acting like he was white, and they said, 'He's forgotten his ABCs. I thought they meant first initials, but in their language it meant Always Be Coloured, and they let me in on all that. It was so exciting. To me that was the greatest accolade.

They had their quota of shits, but those who were good were better than the whites because they had to be. They had to be stronger, more loyal, more committed, because they had nothing to lose and a lot to gain.

We elected the first black New York City councillor, Benjamin Davis Jr. I had a wonderful time.

In the mid-1930s at the beginning of the US women's

movement, I was already fighting on two fronts: for my right to be equal to the men in the Party, and against racism. I saw the men were all political activists and they didn't type, so I refused to learn to type and became an activist too!

Around that time I discovered Sojourner Truth, the first black American slave woman orator to speak out against slavery. She epitomizes the struggle against racism, sexism; and the inspiration she gave me kept me tied to what I call my noble cause.

What kind of inspiration?

Being a communist wasn't easy. Within the Party — which I love and has given me everything I have today — there were warts. But she gave me strength. Nothing could divert her; she gave me that sense, 'You stick in there, kid. You stay committed. You believe in this? To hell with everyone who's messing you about!' And I was being messed about. I was a young, attractive sex object!

I became very aware of sexism, and used a Marxist phrase about economics from *Das Kapital* to describe men, 'Men have a limited use value!' which I exploited most satisfactorily. But the male ego is hopeless, and now I feel sorry for men. They are victims too. One way or another men and women are both victims.

I aspired to be like Sojourner Truth even though she was taller! She was my first real inspiration, because of her courage against the unbelievable and her determination — the things she had to overcome. Here was a woman without education, a slave who became this great orator, organizer. The courage of this woman, putting her life on the line for others constantly.

This woman should be lauded everywhere in the world. Somehow, until she was briefly resurrected by the international women's movement, ten years ago, Sojourner Truth had been thoroughly forgotten. She is one of the great historical figures and most of the people I mention her to, even good left-wingers and comrades, have never heard of her. It kills me. When are we going to give Sojourner Truth her proper place in history? The work she did in the fields, carried stuff better than men. She was head and shoulders above many men.

Who exactly was she?

Her real name was Isabella Baumfree. She was born a slave in Ulster County, New York State, US, 1777, and belonged to several owners. Her slave name was Van Wagener, taken from the last of a series of owners, Isaac Van Wagener, who set her free in 1827, just before the state abolished slavery.

She had several children by Thomas, a fellow slave, and the first thing she did as a free woman was fight through the court under a New York law banning slavery, to recover and free her son who'd been sold illegally into the American South.

In 1829, Isabella Van Wagener, as she was known, went to New York with her two youngest children and worked for 10 or 15 years as a domestic. Eventually she joined up with Elijah Pierson, a zealous religious missionary, and became a street preacher.

In 1843, aged 46, the same year she was introduced to the abolitionism of slavery, she was 'commanded by voices' to take the name Sojourner Truth. She became an evangelist and spoke at revival meetings in eastern States. She was a tall, gaunt figure, with piercing eyes and spoke with a heavy Dutch accent. She never learned to read or write, but she had a natural eloquence and great personal magnetism. Her deep, resonant voice, a quick wit and inspiring faith in God electrified her audiences and this led to some misgivings as to whether she was indeed a woman at all! There were repeated attempts by male mobs to silence her, but this only spurred her on.

Her early speeches were based on the belief that people could best show their love for God by their love and active concern for others, and soon she directed her speeches towards the abolition of slavery.

In 1850 she dictated her biography, prefaced first by William Lloyd Garrison, and later by Harriet Beecher Stowe. She supported herself by odd jobs and by selling her biography, while lecturing all over the country on the abolition of slavery and, increasingly, on the suffrage issue, and union causes.

Her fame spread to Washington and President Lincoln appointed her counsellor to the freed black men of Washington. She worked to improve the living conditions for blacks in Washington and she helped find jobs and homes for slaves escaping from the South to Washington. She promoted a plan to the Grant administration, under which the Federal Government was to set aside undeveloped lands in the West as farms for blacks — a Negro state. But the plan was not supported by the Government. Nevertheless, she encouraged a substantial migration of freed men to Kansas and Missouri.

At the beginning of the US Civil War, Sojourner Truth integrated
Washington streetcars and during the Civil War she visited soldiers
in camp, dispensing gifts and spiritual guidance.

Sojourner Truth encountered women's rights in 1850 or 1851.
She attended the first US national women's rights convention in
Worcester, Massachussetts, the Akron Women's Rights
Convention. In her speech she characterized slave women as 'The
most grossly outraged of the entire sex.' She went on, 'If de first
woman God ever made was strong enough to turn de world
upside down all alone, dese women togedder oughta be able to
turn it back, and get it right side up again. An now dey's asking
to do it, de men better let 'em.' [Ibid]

She retired in 1875 and, aged nearly 100, died November 26th
1883 in Battle Creek, Michigan, her last home.

When did you decide to become a communist and why?

As well as wanting to fight racial discrimination, during the
Depression I started to become aware the government was
dumping food in the ocean when millions were starving. I thought
to myself, 'What kind of insane world am I living in?' And it's
the same today. We have food mountains and people in the under-
developed countries are starving. We have Band Aid, Sport Aid,
yet it's the same circle in this stupid society.

The third factor was the Spanish Civil War, the Popular Front.
The first struggle against fascism, I was inspired by that. All kinds
of people were involved; rich, poor, but of course the Left lead
it by recruiting people to go to Spain and fight facist Franco.

Also, it was the time of the Scottsborough youth trials. Nine
young black men in the South were serving prison sentences for
having intercourse with two white prostitutes on a train. During
the great depression people were travelling all over looking for
work, jumping and riding the freight cars. They were caught, it
was in the South and it was Communist lawyers that went down
to defend them. This inspired me as well.

It was such an exciting time. Because of their role in the Spanish
Civil War, the Communist Party was very big in those days, always
in the lead. All kinds of people were involved, including
Hollywood stars. So, although my father was a socialist, a lovely
sweet man, very gentle (my mother was a dynamo, not political,
and worshipped my father), I had terrible arguments with my

father when I became a Communist, because the Socialists and Communists hated each other's guts. It's like the feminist sisterhood — we tear each other apart instead of tearing the system apart.

A lot of my friends were joining. Anyone with any intelligence went towards the Communist Party and, interestingly, I've been told the same thing was happening in the UK around the same time. In fact, when I arrived here 34 years ago, the Party met every Tuesday night, the same as in the States!

Why did you come to England?

Charlie was my third husband, the first two didn't last very long! How I got involved with British men I'll never know, me a New York working class girl! My first husband was British; tall, blonde, handsome and a great raconteur; almost twice my age. All the girls made a play for him. Years later they said to me, 'Thank God

Sojourner Truth. Reproduced courtesy of Mary Evans/Fawcett Library.

you won!' He was a womanizer, head in the clouds, get-rich-quick
schemes. We were on the dole. He gave me my two nice children,
then we got divorced and I married my second husband, another
womanizer.

Thank God the Second World War came in between so he was
in Europe for a few years. He came back and it was hell. Those
two husbands put me through hell. I was a very jealous, insecure
young woman. I fell for all the magazine bullshit of the ideal man,
the ideal love and all that, and then I discovered there was no
such thing. I learned everything the hard way. We separated and
a few days later I met Charlie.

We fell madly in love. He was a good comrade, separated from
his wife for nine years, and I was a good comrade. He had been
a top trade union official, but it was the MacCarthy period, which
stretched from 1948 to 1953.

He was one of the founders of the Congress of Industrial
Organizations, which in the 1930s organized millions of workers
into this new trade union because the only other trade union
congress was based on skilled craftsmen only. They weren't
interested in unskilled labour.

Eventually Charlie became International Vice President of the
Gas, Coke and Chemical Workers Union in the Niagara Falls area.
He was a brilliant organizer, but the Cold War, and McCarthyism
meant he was in and out of prison for his beliefs between 1948
and 1953. They were passing terrible laws, like the infamous Walter
McCarren Act, under which you could be deported.

Charlie was born in Scotland. He'd tried to become a US citizen,
but they'd always stalled him because he was well-known as a
left-winger, a Communist and top trade union official. A week
before his deportation, the lawyers got word that he would be
deported to Britain. Charlie had become a father to my son and
daughter. We were very close and I had to make this terrible
decision to stay or go. I decided to go with Charlie and I ran around
like a blue-arsed fly, packed two suitcases and a trunk, and left
everything else, including my house and home.

Charlie was brought to the ship handcuffed by two FBI guys
and locked up in the hold for four hours when the ship sailed,
until we were out of US waters. Then he was released.

We arrived here December 2nd, 1953. Things were still rough.
It was the austerity years following the war and we were rationed
to two shillings' worth of meat a week each. It was murder. We'd
never felt anything in the States — a bit of rationing but I could

always get my cigarettes. We never went without. We had a hard time the first two years. My son stayed in the States and married very young. My daughter followed us, lived here for three years, then went back to America for a holiday, stayed and married.

The Party was a good Party when we arrived; it was big, like a huge international family. We had great credentials from the US. We were the first MacCarthyite victims and it made Britain feel superior. We got a great deal of favourable publicity. It was most unusual because Britain was going through one of its anti-American wealth phases — the three big Os: they're overpaid, oversexed and over here! There was a lot of stuff about the GI brides and the horrors that some of them went through back in the States. Even the right wing press made us their darlings because it made Britain look more democratic, which it was. There was more room for eccentrics, and Communists were considered eccentric.

I wanted to become integrated here. I didn't want to be an ex-pat American. A small group of Hollywood ex-pats living in Hampstead, with plenty of money, tried to involve us. They were friendly, good left-wingers, blacklisted and persecuted by the FBI, but they spent a lot of time bemoaning what they were missing and Charlie and I didn't want to get involved in all that.

I miss my kids but I've built my life here, and when Charlie died four years ago, everyone asked if I'd go back. I thought about it but I've been here 31 years. I've made it here, I've grown old here. If I went back I'd be a stateless person. I've tried to keep up with what's going on there and I went back last year and suffered culture shock, good and bad.

What did you do when you arrived?

Charlie went to work in Battersea power station for eight pounds a week as a labourer. He was magnificent, never a word of complaint. He did the filthiest jobs. The man was already in his 50s. He had this brilliant mind. He took a correspondence course in turbine-driven engines, and corrected the text books! He was a natural leader of men and so committed, so singleminded fighting for better conditions. In six months he became Chairman of the Works Committee in the trade union at Battersea Power Station, the biggest power station in Europe at that time.

I spent the first year travelling up and down the country speaking about the resistance to McCarthyism. There was a blackout on news of any struggle against it. All you got was stories about people going to prison, being deported. I went around talking about the fact we were fighting back and I got a wonderful reception wherever I went. At the same time there was a group of musicians, left-wingers, called The People's Artists, who were black and white. Pete Seeger was among them. They gave me records of all kinds of folk songs with social messages. On one of the records Laura Duncan, a black woman, sang 'We Shall Overcome'. We were singing it long before it became the protestors' anthem.

I began to incorporate this music in my meetings. I would introduce each record because each record was political. It made lovely evenings. The cold, reserved English would come up at the end and throw their arms around me. It was a wonderful year, except we didn't eat very well and we froze to death with only coal fires. I was used to central heating! It was quite a culture shock.

A year later I decided, 'I gotta go work in a factory.' I'd been preaching the industrial proletariat all these years and never been inside a factory. I quit school early and the Party educated me. I was pregnant when I was 16 and I'd never really worked, except for the Party.

So I went to work in an engineering factory with 800 women and 400 men. It was wild! I didn't know the body had so many muscles. Charlie had to roll me out of bed every morning, swollen from head to foot. The speed we worked from 8 a.m. to 6 p.m.; operating lathes, making aerials. Time and motion men would come around and speed us up. That film, *Modern Times*, with Charlie Chaplin — that was me, kid! And all those women! I was Rosie the Rivetter. I rivetted, I lathed, and I earned a smart five pounds a week. To me it was a short cut towards getting to know the British working class women. I discovered I couldn't understand what they were saying. I thought Americans spoke the same language, but we didn't.

Once I got accepted — which wasn't easy when they found out I was a Communist and a Yank, and according to them, an intellectual — there was never a dull moment. Their wit! They were beasts of burden; they had three or four kids, they'd get up in the morning, do all the housework (the husbands did nothing), and their humour, their survival . . . It was a link back to Sojourner Truth's day — nowhere near what she went through — but in the same way they worked themselves to death and never lost their humour, their excitement about living. It was great.

The camaraderie was so wonderful. Of course there were pockets of bitterness, but the majority were wonderful. They helped one another long before the consciousness-raising of the women's movement. It was like one big extended family. They inspired me as human beings.

After three years I began to organize them, trying to improve their working conditions. Then one day the company locked me out and wouldn't let me in. The lousy right wing union didn't fight for me so I was sacked. I came home and I, who never cried, burst into tears.

You were both on low pay. How did you cope?

We had enough to live on; we could eat, we had enough heat. We didn't do without. It was the first three years that were rough. Charlie was earning eight pounds, I was earning five. We had a mortgage, bought furniture on the instalment plan. From this tiny joint income we were paying out on all sides. We had nothing when we arrived, a few clothes and a trunkful of books. What an idiot I was! After a few days Charlie sat me down and said, 'We can't both be working class heroes. One of us has to start earning decent money. Who's it gonna be, you or me?' We kicked it around and decided it would be me.

What did you decide to do?

Well, I'd written thousands of leaflets for the Party in my time, and I was a compulsive reader. So I bluffed my way into advertising, as an American. I went from strength to strength; I was earning big money. I was a copywriter and became copy chief. We could eat well, we redecorated, bought a car and new furniture.

I moved from agency to agency, staying in each for two-and-a-half years. It was musical chairs. Creative people would switch jobs just to get more money. You got bored writing about the same products. But it killed me to see Charlie working shift work 12 hours a day in Battersea power station, earning £18 a week. I was getting £50 a week; teachers were making £23. It was insanity! Three-hour expense account lunches, getting pissed, sleeping on your desk unable to work! But I loved the sophistication and the humour among those drunken colleagues of mine.

I had to lie about my age. I was 50 but said I was 34, otherwise I'd never have got a job. The maximum age in advertising is 35. I had to reduce the age of my kids; I couldn't talk about them. After three months, I'd tell them I'd lied about my age, I'm really 41! They think at 51 you can't think anymore or be creative. Hell, I was a good copywriter! I understood the market, I had a feeling about what people wanted, I knew how to sell, I was good with words and slogans.

I used to meet with another Communist, a man, and we'd compare the jargon. Each lunchtime every week we ended up saying, 'If you can sell Communism, you can sell anything!' And we did. He did very well and so did I. I had my nightmares about doing things the wrong way, but I did OK.

When did you become a journalist?

One day I was dragged to an Communist Embassy reception, and I met the then Editor of the *Morning Star*. He asked what was I doing. I said, 'I'm between jobs because I'm expecting my daughter and her sons to come on a visit and I want to be with them.' He began to pressure me, so I said, 'I'm not a journalist. I can't type, but I'll be Woman's Page editor for three months.' Their gross pay was £15 a week. I was paying more than that in taxes.

I was back to my working class earnings, but I loved it; the page and the women I met. I never stopped travelling up and down the country lecturing at trade union schools, university socialist societies, the right wing yelling at me. I loved it. I stayed on the *Morning Star* for 18 years.

You've never sacrificed your principles?

No. No, I'd never, ever do that. I try to live according to my principles and I've more or less succeeded throughout my life. I know I'm not perfect, I've weaknesses and faults, but I can look at myself in the mirror and say, 'You're not a bad human being.' I can say it with full confidence, now I'm approaching 72.

Looking back on my mistakes, I've always been honest, except when I lied about my age to the ad agencies. I was never in competition with anyone. To me, people are fascinating and interesting; it makes you care about them. Outside of the few baddies that I came across — and they're everywhere — people have the potential for both good and bad. I have a shit list; I hate hypocrisy. Give me an honest enemy. I can cope with that, but I hate two-faced people.

Most of my friends are young; I don't know if that's a weakness or not. I've decided not to analyse it, but they keep me alive and they love me because they've got an unmoralizing, experienced woman to pour their troubles out to. I'm a sounding board for them. I'm still interested in what's happening now. I'm involved in what's happening now and these young people, mostly women, are giving me today. I'm from yesterday. I play devil's advocate. In my youth I was an adviser, but I don't give advice any more, I can't make decisions for other people. I'm like a psychiatrist, except that I don't charge anything! And a feminist one. It's a wonderful combination I give to them and they give back to me. It's the give and take of those friendships that keeps me going. I need to be needed.

Do or did you find making yourself and your needs a top priority difficult?

Essentially I've lived a fascinating, very enriching, wonderful life. I made fun out of everything I did. I had to have humour in the most horrible situations, boring Party meetings every week. We never took enough time out for the fun.

I have no regrets, except one. I should have taken a little more time off to do what I wanted to do. I always made time for sex, which was very enjoyable most of the time, except for those first two duds.

Too many women are like me, guilt ridden about the kids, the husband, the partner, the job. We're too responsible for everything. We are the carers, givers. Working together, we ought to organize more social events for ourselves but we've not learned how to do that yet. We don't know how to enjoy ourselves. We have our laughs at the meetings, but we never take time off. We sacrifice our personal lives to our work.

Even now I find it difficult to put myself first. I'm still caught up in the frenzy. I go to parties I don't enjoy, I get home exhausted and I think that's not really what I want. I'd like to give or go to dinner parties where there's plenty of drink, a good discussion, and a loving atmosphere, even though we might fight with each other passionately. To me that's lovely.

I would like to go to the theatre more often, concerts, which

I love, but the Movement has swallowed me up. Anything can swallow you up.

I don't feel burned out, I feel old and sick, but I still fight, travel, give talks. But I've slowed down; I work at my own pace. That's great. If I didn't I'd be dead. I don't take time off but I'm telling everybody else to!

This last six months I've been saying to my friends, 'Listen! This is Granny Doyle. Take time off for yourself. Indulge yourself, because life is short. It goes so fast that before you know it you'll be 72 years old and sick like me.' Tomorrow I might not wake up. I hope I go that way when I have to go. But I'm at the age when most of my peers have died and I've come to terms with the fact I'm not going to live forever.

How do you manage your anger and what makes you angry?

Any kind of injustice. It's important to get angry; it makes the adrenalin flow. But anger isn't enough; it's got to be channelled and directed to bring about change.

I'm a fighter. I will speak out, drag my arse somewhere, even though I'm half dead, tired and don't feel like going. I'll go speak and fight because I'm directing my anger against those who have the power to inflict injustice. They must always be challenged. Don't turn the other cheek to the infliction of injustice on others, regardless of race, colour, sex, creed, whatever. I may not agree with that person but if they're unjustly treated, I'm on their side fighting for them. That's been my principle all my life.

How do you cope with failure? Give me an example of when you failed and you coped with it?

I felt I failed when they wouldn't let me in to the factory. That was a terrible failure. I failed to get back in. Three years of hard slog went out the window.

One guy I couldn't get when I was 15. He was a tall, handsome Italian. He didn't want me. He was the only man I couldn't get in my whole life. I was heartbroken and I suffered.

You keep trying, but there comes a point of no return and you suffer. You hate yourself, you examine yourself, life becomes unbearable for a while, but then you discover the in-built will to survive.

To encourage young people fed up with failing I say, 'Don't give up. You throw a pebble in a pool and it ripples. You don't know where it'll end, but you must keep on throwing those pebbles in the pool.' To me this is scientific.

I remember trying to understand Nazism and fascism. I read all the stuff I could lay my hands on, including the reports on concentration camps and the atrocities committed. I learned there were many suicides in Nazi Germany, but they were mainly the upper classes; the working class decided to fight.

They had little to lose; the very act of surviving gives you a particular kind of strength. The people with a lot to lose are victims of their own circumstances. They never develop that inner strength you find among black people or working class people. They develop this inner strength in order to survive in a world that has kept them down in terms of education and opportunity. You learn to live with the pain for a while and then it goes. You bleed, you're wounded, but you heal. It takes variable amounts of time, depending on the depth of the wound, but scar tissue is tougher than the original skin! You get over pain, you survive.

For me, my greatest survival mechanism was my ability to stand back and laugh at myself and life generally. I take my commitment seriously but I've learned not to take myself so seriously. I might be at someone's throat, but eventually there'll be a laugh. It's the same with failure. You live with it and you push it away.

Is being a woman an intrinsic part of your work?

Yes. It means doing things my way. As a result of being a woman, our raised awareness, and the women's movement, I think I've brought about a compassion and a sensitivity to the feelings and sufferings of others. This compassion is a special contribution that women have to give in every sphere of life and activity. It's missing in parliaments, in business, everywhere, and sadly some women who've broken through and made it into the male domain become one of the boys. But they are victims too. I don't sit in judgment on them. I feel sorry for them.

I feel sorry for men as well. Bill Morris, the only black top trade union official — a nice guy — has a terrible burden. I've heard him called an Uncle Tom. He may not be for black sections, but he's been used; he has to present his union's views. They may not be his, he's just stuck with it. But it's a beginning. There'll be more black trade unionists in the same way as there are now black MPs. What a breakthrough that's been!

I'll fight for the token woman or token black because it is a breakthrough. But let's not stop there. You can't sit back; we have to keep battling on.

When do you feel most vulnerable?

When we had that awful storm in the autumn of 1987, I felt very vulnerable with 100-mile-an-hour winds blowing down all the trees, electricity pylons. My home's all electric — a big mistake — and we had a power cut for seven-and-a-half hours. A friend woke me, telephoning to find out if I was all right. She lived far away and I couldn't say, 'No. I'm not all right,' but I was very touched that she phoned.

I sat here thinking, 'I must have a cup of coffee first thing in the morning.' Half an hour later, a young woman appeared at my front door. She'd walked from work with a big thermos flask of hot water. I burst into tears. No-one ever sees me cry; I do it in private. All my life while everyone else at the movies cries at suffering, cruelty, I'll sit stony faced, but when happiness or achievement is on the screen I'll cry my eyes out. Kindness breaks me up. Achievement, overcoming incredible odds, tears me to pieces. I was so happy and touched that she remembered in the midst of all the chaos that my house was all electric. I don't know her that well, either. I kept calling her the good fairy! I felt very vulnerable.

And since Charlie died four years ago, I've read about 86-year-olds getting raped. I'm alone in this house. Raped at 86 by a 20-year-old! God, that is so sick! So I've made my flat more secure and I have an extension phone next to my bed. I was very scared until I'd done that.

I'm going to spend every penny I've got on travelling before I die. But it's hard for old women to travel. If you're a man you can get away with murder. Everywhere you go you're made welcome. But a single woman, no way! Being a woman alone makes me feel extra vulnerable. Society isn't ready for the extra or the single woman. No matter how intelligent, loveable, charming or fun you might be, you're a woman and they don't want extra women at the dinner party table.

How can it be made better?

People must be more sensitive to the needs of women alone. There are a great many of us, all ages. We still have a long way to go in the understanding of women as a separate entity. An extra woman at a dinner party is a pain in the arse, no matter how attractive your personality. An extra man is totally acceptable. I probably get more invitations than most old women, but even I get forgotten. It's very hurtful. As little as it happens, it's still too much. A couple of years ago, a group of us single women did something about it. We got together for Christmas. You need money to do it of course, but it's a wonderful idea if you don't have a partner, family, and you're alone. Even in the women's movement, we have a long way to go in overcoming the peculiar situation that this culture and society has put women on their own into.

What are you most proud of?

I was proud of myself when I got into advertising and found I could earn the big bucks. I quit school when I was 13, and I thought it was quite an achievement competing successfully with highly educated university graduates and becoming a copy chief.

I am proud of the fact I can teach, inform and communicate with all kinds of professionals at all kinds of different levels, be they lawyers, teachers, whoever.

I am proud of the fact I have so many very good friends. It makes me feel good that they care about me and we're close. It's an equal relationship. I'm proud that I can give them love and receive it.

We all have the potential for good and bad and I'm proud I can bring out the good in people.

I'm proud of my objectivity — about myself as well as others. If you're honest and don't kid yourself you reach a moment of truth with yourself as you mature.

I'm proud of my unswerving commitment. We may have advanced things over the years, but I don't believe we'll ever attain true equality,until we have socialism, although I know women are still unequal in socialist countries and old attitudes die hard. But I wouldn't dream of bringing that up at a meeting, imposing my beliefs on anyone even when I've stood alone voting against something, because right now we're all fighting to advance

women's status, interests, opportunities, and very often I quickly
find myself no longer standing alone.

Right now I'm locked in a dire battle with the British
Communist Party leadership and its policies. I'm in total
disagreement with everything they're doing. It's been going on
a long time, getting more and more dire. The Party is killing itself;
we're tearing each other to pieces. It's very tragic at a time now
when we need good leadership . . . but we're going to pay for
it, the whole world will pay for it.

Do you have a sense of your own spirituality?

I've always called myself a materialist in the Marxist sense and
I'm a totally committed atheist. I can't put it in Marxist terms,
but some Communists are different from other Communists. We
should all be the same, we share the same beliefs, but why do
I feel closer to some Tories than I do to some of my own
comrades? I have a great friend, a member of the aristocracy. We
went to Moscow together. She has guilt feelings about her wealth;
she's a Caltholic and a true believer in her faith. She is so devout.
She prays every day, yet she insists I'm the most religious person
she's met. We're very close and known as thc 'odd couple'! It's
taken me many years to understand what she meant. I used to
say it's a chemical thing, but it's more than that. I don't know
if spirituality is the right word, but for want of something better
it must be that; an essence, vibes you give off.

I think my spirit will live on in the world in a smaller way, like
the spirit of Sojourner Truth which left its mark on me.

Do you have a personal vision?

Oh, yes. It's kept me going all these years. It's a world in which
we eliminate poverty and there are no more wars; a world where
people really care about each other, people are equal, and different
— not the same. I want dignity for every human being to take
away all the evils in the history of the world from the time it started.
That's my Utopian dream; that's what I work towards. A world
where people care about each other and live with dignity and
in peace. It'll take a long time to get it the way I'd like it to be.
I know I'm not going to see it, but I have confidence that some
day it will come, because the potential for good in people is there.

I saw it when I first came here. The Second World War bomb

sites blew my mind. I was horrified at what the Londoners and others in Britain had suffered. But everyone spoke with nostalgia about it; they cared about each other. Sadly it disappeared after the war. Nowadays, it's, 'I'm all right, Jack!' But I know, given the proper conditions, and time, that goodness will some day come out again. I've lived my life by the determination to bring it about as quickly as I can. Now I've come to the realization I ain't gonna see it, it's the legacy of hope I'll leave — I hope.

Mary Stott. Reproduced courtesy of the *Guardian*.

Mary Stott

Journalist

Indirectly, Mary's innovative, trendsetting journalism and editorship of the Guardian's *women's pages in the '60s and '70s had a significant impact on the development of the women's movement in Britain. Now in her 80s, Mary's rather fed up talking about herself, but I was glad she agreed in the end because she's someone I admire tremendously.*

Did you always want to be a journalist?

Originally I wanted to take a high-powered secretarial course so that I could go to Geneva and work for the League of Nations, but my mother and father were both journalists and when I talked to them after I had written an essay on newspapers for school, it was like a call to the ministry; nothing else would do from that point on.

My first job came as a result of my mother helping out her brother when he had staffing troubles on the *Leicester Mail*, where he was chief sub-editor. I think she was the first female sub-editor on a British newspaper and almost certainly the first on a provincial newspaper. When I'd made up my mind that's what I wanted to do, she marched into the editor's office, said, 'What about my daughter?' and he took me on. I was 17.

I was extremely lucky to have such a persuasive person for my mother — not a bossy-boots in a disagreeable way, but she could charm the birds from the trees. She always got what she wanted in a good cause.

I never worked in Fleet Street. I spent all my working life in and around Manchester. I came to the *Guardian* in Gray's Inn Road just two years before I retired.

I stayed for six years with the *Leicester Mail*. It was owned by the Leicester Tory Party and the main shareholder was Sir Arthur Wheeler, a stockbroker who failed in business. Consequently, the paper got into disastrous financial difficulties and a number of us were fired, including me. It wasn't because I was inefficient, but my mother had just died and everyone thought I'd better stay at home and look after my father!

Fortunately my father wasn't that kind of person. He helped me to find a job in Bolton, Lancashire and I stayed in the north. It was 1931, right in the depths of the Depression. In 1933 I became the editor of the women's and children's publications of the Co-operative Movement. I stayed there for about 15 years.

That was a most important time in my life. I learned to communicate with people without much education. It was wonderful; they were marvellous women. So positively orientated towards social welfare, peace — very strongly pacifist — which suited me down to the ground. I was a pacifist, like many others, because of the horrible slaughter of the First World War. (It was my desire to work for peace that lead me to think about working for the League of Nations in Geneva.)

What exactly were you doing?

I didn't only edit the magazine, I was responsible for all the layouts, which I greatly enjoyed, and during the war I handled the news pages of the Co-operative News. That's one of the things I most liked doing — handling the news. I always wanted to be a sub-editor. Later, I got the opportunity of doing just that at the *Manchester Evening News*, then the financial supporter of its sister paper, the *Manchester Guardian*. That, too, was a high spot. It was in many ways exactly what I wanted: very fast, quick; handling the news all day long with very few pauses. I enjoyed that enormously. That came to an end because I really should have been promoted and then the editor said, 'No. We have to safeguard the succession, and the successor has to be a man.' He actually used those words! I felt absolutely dreadful and left, not out of pique but because I knew I had no future there. It would have meant staying till I was a granny, teaching young men my job and before I knew where I was they'd be in charge. I just wouldn't do it. I had natural pride in my craft and skills. I don't think any man would have done it.

I stayed at home and looked after my daughter for a bit, then went back to the Co-operative Press part-time with a slightly different standing — I'd seen and proved myself in the wider world of journalism. I was made very welcome by the Guildswomen as well as by the Co-operative Press and was invited to speak at Co-operative Women's Guild meetings and at their national congress. That showed me they thought I was a person worth having.

In 1957 Alistair Hetherington, editor of the *Guardian*, gave me the chance to edit the women's page. I was delighted. I grew up with the *Guardian* and *Time and Tide*; they were a great resource, an inspiration to me. It was the only women's page I would ever have considered editing.

Vera Brittain and Winifred Holtby wrote for it regularly before the war. After the war, the then editor turned it over to a man with a clutch of other things under his arm; travel, letters to the editor, anything that nobody else wanted to do. He ran a good page, three days a week. I was officially his assistant. We practically never met because I left at 3 p.m. to collect my daughter from school and he started at 4 p.m. We communicated with little notes; it was most agreeable, without any tension. He was a good comrade. Although he was supposed to be a bit spikey, I never found him so

I was editor from 1957 to 1972. Up until the early '60s the women's page was only three days a week. Then *The Times* started a daily women's page and we had to keep up. It really took off. It makes me laugh now; it was often at the bottom of the page on a Monday underneath the motoring column — motoring was deemed far more important than women's issues in those days!

It wasn't the writing, but the stuff that came in the post that gave me most pleasure; articles written by non-professional women about their own experience. They had such a wonderful freshness and were so genuine. I remember a features editor saying I ought to use more professional stuff. I said, 'No. The personal experience articles are the best thing about the page.' He said, 'But journalists have personal experiences.' I said, 'Yes, but they come out differently.' In the nicest possible way I think journalists write for effect. Non-professionals write because they are driven to it.

There was the famous Betty Thorne, living in a two-up-two-down in Sheffield. She wrote marvellously, in kids' lined notebooks. Her articles really gave the flavour of life in a back street in Sheffield.

It's the 'do-it-yourself decade' that's remembered now —
organizations that sprang up because someone's letter or article
sparked off action: The National Association for the Welfare of
Children in Hospital, the Disabled Incomes Group, Pre-school
Playgroups Association; people say if I'd not been there it wouldn't
have happened. That may be so — I don't know. I was very thrilled
that they did happen but in fact I did get most pleasure from the
personal experience pieces. They weren't always jolly either. One
woman wrote about her son becoming a heroin addict.

Who was your greatest inspiration?

I think the most inspiring influence on my own life was Mary
Stocks who I knew personally and who became Baroness Stocks
of the Royal Borough of Kensington and Chelsea. She would
choose a title like that! One of the marvellous things about Mary
was her incredible sense of fun. She was frightfully funny and
probably one of the best known people on the radio programme
Any Questions. One Saturday at lunch time I was in the bedroom
with my husband changing for some do or other and suddenly
we were rolling about the bed laughing at something Mary Stocks
had said.

She was a dedicated feminist and an extremely able woman,
and to my way of thinking, stunningly beautiful. I'm not in the
least bit touched by the Marilyn Monroe kind of beauty, the curves,
roundness and the sexiness. Mary Stocks had a very austere beauty.
That's what really moves me; I can sit and watch a face like that
for ever. Strangely, she must somehow in her upbringing have
lost confidence in her appearance. Maybe she had beautiful
relations or friends who made her feel inadequate, I don't know.
She didn't take any interest in her clothes; she was quite dowdy.
I remember once seeing her on a platform put her hand up her
skirt and pull a handkerchief out of her bloomers! When she
became an old lady she took to wearing elegant trouser suits
which made her look very handsome. Tall, thin, striding about,
she had an androgenous air about her. She always wore her hair
short — a neat crop. It was her intellectual beauty that appealed
to me.

I first met her when I was working on the *Bolton Evening News*.
There was a meeting of the local Women's Citizen's Association
to discuss what was then called birth control, and Mary Stocks
was the chief speaker. The meeting was invaded by great bus loads

of Catholic women and their priests from Salford, who practically broke up the meeting. It was extraordinary, the savage attacks made on women of that kind in the early 1930s. But Mary Stocks was always brave and perfectly calm.

It was she who set up a birth control clinic in 1926 in Greengate, Salford with two other very dear friends of mine, Charis Frankenburg and Flora Blomberg. They suffered the most dreadful hostility. Ghastly things were said about them, but they felt it was something they simply had to do. They had far more courage than I have. They were practically called painted harlots. It was very funny because each of these pioneers had a very sedate family background with a husband and four children each.

I met Mary Stocks for the first time not long after my mother had died. I was very lonely and feeling my way in my new life in the north. I think the only way to deal with grief is to do something new. I went to a workers' education class in Salford — nineteenth century economic history — and Mary Stocks was the teacher. I did so enjoy those classes; they were enormously stimulating. I remember quite a lot of what she told me to this day and that's 50 years ago. She was a wonderful lecturer. Later on, after her husband, Professor J.R. Stocks died, she became Principal at Westfield College. She wrote frequently for the *Guardian* and other journals but the broadcasting came fairly late in her life. I don't remember her talking specifically on feminist issues very much but she wrote articles, books and a biography of Eleanor Rathbone, who fought for 25 years for child allowances. Mary Stocks was in the same mould as Miss Rathbone. I really don't know why I'm so aware she was a feminist, but her attitude towards equality of the sexes was almost exactly the one I've adopted.

My definition of a feminist is a person who wholeheartedly believes in equality of the sexes, as the Fawcett Society puts it, in law, custom and practice. They are prepared to say so publicly and do something practical about it — join a committee or whatever. A feminist is not a battling person, all anti-men; that's not what I call feminism. Our nineteenth century foremothers were feminists. You'd be quite surprised how early it came into their vocabulary.

Mary Stocks was a very active member of the National Union for Women's Suffrage Societies, which after 1918 became the National Union of Societies for Equal Citizenship. I was too young to take an active part in that, but I knew about it.

Baroness Stocks. Reproduced courtesy of Hulton Picture Library.

Come 1928, we got the vote on the same terms as men. I wish
to state here and now I was a Flapper voter and I voted for the
first time in 1929, aged 21. I was one of those 'star turns', and
terribly conscious of it. It was a wonderful day, at least *legally*
we were now on the same footing as men because we had the
vote.

After that achievement, Mary Stocks, with Dame Marjorie
Corbett-Ashby and other excellent women, thought up the idea
of the National Union of Townswomen's Guilds. They said to
themselves, 'There are all these millions of women voters, without
much experience or knowledge of how the system works, and
they ought to be encouraged to train themselves as citizens.' There
were also lots of women about the country who had campaigned
marvellously for suffrage now 'out of a job', needing something
else to do.

The Townswomen's Guilds modelled themselves on the rural
Women's Institutes but they were only in towns 'big enough to
support a Woolworths'! Although they had crafts sections, the
emphasis was much more on understanding how government
worked at local and national level. They had public affairs sections,
lectures and discussions. It was a fine organization and still is.
Splendid people like Mary Stocks and Marjorie Corbett-Ashby
started it and were the motivating force behind its success.

You can see why Mary inspired me. She was highly intelligent,
with a deep interest in public affairs. She was the epitome of what
I wanted to achieve. Of course I knew I didn't have her intellect
but she led the sort of public life that I would have liked to copy.
She was rather austere, though very likeable and frightfully funny.
She was probably more reserved than I am. She got things going
and that's what I like to do; bring people together, stick my fingers
in the pie, stir things up and see what comes of it.

In my later years at the *Guardian* in Manchester, I became quite
friendly with Lady Simon of Wythenshawe, a very strong-minded,
powerful lady, one-time chairman of Manchester City Council
Education Committee. She was a real power in the land and often
asked me to supper — and always when Mary Stocks came to
stay with her. That was an enormous thrill to me. We weren't what
I call personal friends but we could talk very easily about all the
issues that interested us both. Her son used to live near me in
Blackheath, in the Paragon, and once Mary's daughter-in-law asked
me to lunch when she was visiting there and we had a super
discussion about Anthony Trollope — we were both devotees.

We had a lot in common but I was always a little wary of intruding in her life. She was 10 or 15 years older than me, which seemed a lot, and her great distinction made me shy of her. I didn't see much of her in her last years as she became very frail and preferred to stay nearer home. She had a dry kind of verbal wit, rather than anecdotal. I received a letter from her in reply to my congratulations on having been elevated to the peerage. (People often used to confuse us because of the similarity of our names.) Mary Stocks wrote: 'Congratulations to me began "Dear Mrs Stott" and I am sure that you will enjoy my title when I have one.'

Have you had to compromise very much in your life, being a woman?

When I was a news sub-editor I should have been appointed a deputy chief sub-editor. If I'd been a man I would have been, without any question at all. That wasn't a compromise, that was a defeat.

It's difficult to assess your own personality, but I don't think I am all that much of a fighter. I would be more likely to sense the atmosphere and withdraw.

My job on the *Guardian* went very much my own way. No-one said I shouldn't do this or that, although I do remember Alistair Hetherington saying something, I don't know what, about my page to the then features editor John Rosselli, and he said, 'Yes, but the page has a very strong personality. Mary mustn't be wooed to do something different; the fact she is doing her own thing on the page is what makes it attractive to readers.' On the whole that was the attitude I experienced. I couldn't say the *Guardian* was ever very sexist, though one thing always makes me laugh: I had an article by Catherine Storr, a very serious writer, on penis envy. Alistair was heard to say that if he'd seen the proof it wouldn't have gone in. He was a very prudish Presbyterian Scot. Compared to the *Guardian* now this article was very tame!

When I came to London, two or three years before I retired, I did feel rather constricted organizationally. It seemed to me that a deputy features editor thought he knew better than I did, though he was much less experienced.

Have you set any goals in your life?

The goals I would like to have achieved, I had no chance of achieving. When I set out in journalism my great ambition was to be a theatre critic. I was mad about the theatre. When I was drafted to the women's page against my wishes they gave me the theatre notices as a kind of sop. I used to love doing that. Above all I think I really would have liked to take charge of a good provincial newspaper and run it with my husband, who was an extremely good sub. (He was night editor and later northern editor on the *News Chronicle*.) But he didn't really want to do that because he worked on a national newspaper and he thought it would have been too parochial. I have a rather different approach to newspapers and I didn't think it would be. I would like to have been in contact with the local community. I don't think I would have liked to run a Fleet Street newspaper; it didn't really appeal to me. But a provincial paper — that was the goal I envisaged even though it was really just a silly dream and there wasn't a hope of it coming true.

Fifteen or so years ago, before I retired, some worthy body gave a lunch for women journalists at the House of Commons and I remember standing up and saying it was probable we would have a woman Prime Minister before we had a woman editor in Fleet Street. I was right!

I don't have any goals now. I write a fortnightly column for the *Liverpool Daily Post* which keeps me going. It's a way of sounding off about things that interest me. I very seldom have to scratch my brains to think of an idea; there are lots boiling up; the next one is already firmly in my head before I've finished the current one. I would like to continue to do a certain amount of journalism both for newspapers and magazines. I hope to go on writing, although I don't want the great labour of doing another book. I've done five and not made money out of any of them. In the case of the *Guardian* anthology, I didn't mind at all because I loved doing it; it was going back over my life. When I was researching that book, one of the first things I read was about Leicester in 1922. Women in the boot and shoe trade were on strike for a wage that brought them up to the men's level. I could remember Mrs Belle Richards, the strike leader, being talked about at home. And do you know, things haven't changed much. That article started by saying a 'sex war' had broken out — that was in 1922!

It's all been done before, but we've still got it to do. People ask me if I think we've got anywhere. Of course we have. We've made enormous advances and we're never going back again. I don't believe in the backlash, it's only a little flicker. Women will never go back to the four walls of their homes. I think the enormous stride was the invention of the Pill. When history is written in the next century I think it will be seen that the introduction of the Pill was what made the crucial difference. Not that I mean all the campaigning hasn't mattered — of course it has. But the Pill enabled women to choose for themselves whether or not to be tied down to a family. All the nineteenth century feminists were supported by their husbands or fathers. I don't denigrate anything they did — I admire them enormously — but they didn't have to earn a living and run a home as well as campaign in their spare time. The Pill means more women can do their own thing, whatever it may be.

What were the lowest times in your life and how did you manage?

The deaths in my family, I think. My husband died on a Tuesday night; the funeral was on Saturday; I went back to work on Monday. What else could I do? That was the way of my life. I had to carry on.

A woman came to talk to me about death recently. I thought she wanted to talk about the hereafter and all that. But she took me through all the deaths in my family and I was absolutely emotionally exhausted at the end. But as I said to her, I came to feel, later on, I had slammed the door too tightly too soon on memories of my husband, but I had to do it. There was no doubt in my mind at the time that I had to go on doing what I was doing, although there was a dreadful sag after three months. When I write to newly widowed people I tell them they have to trudge through the tunnel, hour by hour, day by day, and that one day there'll be a little light. You can't give in.

Of what do you feel most proud?

I get a bit tired of being praised for being around during the 'do-it-yourself' decade of the *Guardian* women's page, but I suppose that's what I feel most thankful to have been associated with. I don't think I feel proud about it, but it's probably what I shall be, and what I should like to be, most remembered for.

How do you enjoy yourself?

Apart from working, I paint and sing in a choir. Well, it's not really singing now, it's more of a croak! Painting, music and gardening, and of course travel — I love going places.

My daughter Catherine organized a birthday present from my family and very old friends — Cook's travel coupons, so now I can think of planning another lovely expedition for the autumn or spring. I'm rather keen to go in February because I think it's a very dismal, depressing month. It's nice to go abroad and get to a warm place. Winter drags on so.

Do you have a personal vision?

A vision of how I would like things to be? I would like men and women to walk hand in hand. I'm not the sort of feminist who thinks women are better than men. I do think we should have more influence on the way things are run but I had a marvellously complete marriage and I think men and women, side by side, can really achieve so much.

I get upset at political hostility. People get so bitter towards one another; it happens in the women's movement. I want to extend the feelings of friendship and comradeship. That's my vision of how the world could be.

Miriam Karlin.

Miriam Karlin OBE

Actress

I met Miriam recovering from moving house and in the middle of a West End production. We met in the theatre foyer and at once a childhood dream came true — going backstage. The stage door hadn't opened, so we groped our way carefully in the dark, along the side of the stage, through the door at the back, up the stairs and into Miriam's dressing room. As usual I was very anxious, but she made me a cup of tea with one of those portable electric red-hot pokers and I soon relaxed.

I come from a middle class orthodox Jewish family. My father, Harry Samuels OBE, was a barrister. My mother was born in Holland and came to England in the First World War. She stayed here and married my father, but unfortunately the rest of the family returned to Holland and eventually were sent to the gas chambers. My father was a brilliant man, with an amazing mind. He was a Greek scholar and wrote a play in Greek when he was 21. My brother, five years my elder, followed an academic life. A Balliol scholar, he's been senior professor of English language at Glasgow University for many years. He's a freak for Middle English and has just published an atlas of Middle English dialects.

It never occurred to me to try for university myself, something I bitterly regret not doing, but I was so eager to get on with acting. They insisted at least I should have a formal training, and I went to RADA.

Have you set yourself specific goals in your life?

My only goal was to act. From the moment I could speak I was doing impersonations! I was five when I saw a Shakespeare play for the first time. My mother took me to see *Midsummer Night's Dream* in Regent's Park, one glorious June afternoon. When I think of total happiness I recapture that moment — I was so joyously happy. I was consciously in love with everything I saw, the ambience, the surroundings, the flowers — I remember the delphiniums were out. It was so beautiful. Sadly, I find as I get older I'm only aware of happiness in retrospect, never at this moment. OK, I enjoy a good dinner, lovely champagne, but it's not the same deep feeling of true happiness.

I used to be taken to pantomimes every year, joined in all the choruses and sang louder than anyone else. Our school arranged visits to the Old Vic; we paid a shilling and sat in the Pit. From the age of seven onwards I saw as much theatre as I could.

I would like the theatre to be as accessible and affordable to young people today as it was when I was young. Children have excessive energy which can go any way, either into beating up somebody or being creative. If I had my way they could channel their energy in the right direction. Self-expression through drama might keep them away from violence.

When I went to RADA, during the Second World War, it was a bit of a joke. It was almost a finishing school for young ladies. All the men were away fighting in the war, so I played all the men's parts. I left RADA in 1945 and from then on it was the usual long, hard slog. In the early days I never turned down a job — I was the dresser, I washed tights, was stage manager, understudy. I did variety, cabaret, almost everything there is in the business, with the exception of circus and ballet. I even did a production of *Fiddler on the Roof* with the Scottish Opera, having been in the original production at Her Majesty's theatre.

What was the attitude of your family and friends to your growing success?

Sheer delight. What else could it have been? Looking back, it was extraordinary that I should get such encouragement to go into the theatre from that sort of family. My father always used to say, 'Oh, she's going to be a second Ruth Draper.' And I have to say, without such amazingly supportive parents, I don't know how I would have survived at the beginning.

I lived at home far longer than most daughters do today. I was comfortable and secure, with a roof over my head and money, so long as I used it to buy food. They had a fit when I started smoking. To boost my income I did the most extraordinary things, but I never took jobs outside acting. I used to flog old school textbooks to Foyles bookshop, and picture frames to actors. One of my father's hobbies was going to auction sales. Amongst the beautiful furniture and works of art there were job lots of ghastly prints which were stacked away in the spare room. It's difficult to understand now, but just after the war it was impossible to find good picture frames and they were terribly expensive. Ours were always rather special and beautifully crafted, so I did a roaring trade selling them to actors for their front of house photographs which, in those days, they were obliged to provide framed.

Although my parents were very supportive, in a way they gave with one hand and took back with the other, because I never really learned what it was to be independent. I'm deeply ashamed to say this, but it took until I was over 50, and my father's death 11 years ago, before I knew I couldn't go crying to Dad for cash anymore. He didn't have pots of money but he was careful and if I had a huge tax bill, he'd always bail me out. He couldn't bear to see me in a state. It was lovely of them to help me but I feel they should have given me more of a sense of financial responsibility. I still haven't got it.

How do you deal with criticism?

It depends from whence it stems! Of course I don't like adverse criticism, but criticism from family and friends is very different from press criticism. When it comes from family and friends I take it very seriously indeed. I might be very upset at the time, arguing, denying and justifying my actions. But normally, I think about what they've said and perhaps three or four months later do a double take and realize they could be right. Then I try to do something about it.

A typical example was when I was in my 20s, doing a weekly revue in Wimbledon with about eight or ten different numbers to learn every week. When there was inefficiency in the theatre and things went wrong, I used to get very upset and scream and swear like a trooper, throwing tantrums all over the place.

The wondrous Evelyn Laye joined us for a few weeks as a guest artist. She called me in to her dressing room one day and said, 'Why do you do it? Why do you throw so many tantrums? Please don't because I think you are *so* talented, but you'll kill yourself and if you cry wolf too often people will just laugh, take no notice.

No-one will want to employ you.' I tried to justify my behaviour
and was really upset that she couldn't understand why I got in
such a state. It was five months before it finally sank in that she
was right. We became very good friends and she told me
she threw a tantrum once every two or three years, '. . . and
when I do, people fly, because they know it's about something
really important.' I won't tolerate inefficiency: bad lighting, dirty
clothes, but I've learned to deal with it without becoming
hysterical.

I've a few close friends who generally criticize me for my *modus
vivendi* — lunacies and obsessions which I realize worsen with
age. But even as a child I've been compulsive over so many things
— dieting, eating. I can't help it; it's ruined my health. My friends
watch me almost trying to kill myself and try to stop me doing
it. I know their criticism is done out of love.

I don't think much of press criticism. I used to rush for
newspapers when I had a first night because I believed what they
said about a performance. If they said I was good, I rejoiced; when
I got a bad notice I went into total despair. There's a very nasty
hurt if you read a bad notice. It took up until the time I joined
the RSC (1981) before I stopped reading notices. I believe the most
important critic is oneself, and I'm the hardest to please.

I suppose it's my age, I can't really take good notices of my
part in an Agatha Christie play seriously when I know I've done
quality work before and it's gone unrecognized. Nevertheless,
it's good to know you've had good notices, even if you don't read
them.

What kind of support do you value most?

My peers'. If I admire and respect a director — and really good
directors are few and far between — and such a director is pleased
with my work, then I'm happy, regardless of what anyone else
says.

I got a big buzz the other day, working on a Yorkshire TV
production called *The Attic* — the story of Miep, the woman who
looked after the Franks when they were in hiding. During the
run of *And Then There Were None*, the theatre management
kindly let me off a couple of performances to go to Yorkshire.

Yesterday morning, John Erman, the director, rang me from
Leeds and said, 'Mim, I watched the rushes last night and I want
to tell you, you were great. I'm so pleased we took the trouble

to organize things so that you could play the part.' He's a talented and highly respected director, and despite being behind schedule he took the time to ring me. That encouragement set me up for the day.

How do you keep going?

In a backhanded way, I think a lot of my energy and strength comes from my campaigning. If I didn't have a campaign I think I would crawl away quietly and die. It's my life's blood. My father was a great campaigner, militant in his own way, and I probably follow in his footsteps.

Have you had to make compromises?

Unless you're working, you can't call yourself an actor. I'm always telling the youngsters to just keep acting, whether it's street theatre, for old people, in schools or community halls — anywhere. And apart from my early career, this is the first time I've taken a theatre job solely for the money. Everyone says there's nothing wrong with that, but I still don't know why I feel such terrible guilt.

I'm riddled with guilt — like most Jewish women. I was brought up with a very strict set of tenets, mores, and if I don't live up to them I'm not perfect, and if you're not perfect, then you feel guilty.

Why do you campaign so much?

I often ask myself that question and worry about my motives. Is it really just for the cause, or do I do it for a buzz and because it makes *me* feel better? I'm a dreadful bore about it, but it bothers me deeply and I have recurrent nightmares about it. The premise is always different but the message is the same.

I remember one dream in which I was deeply concerned that poorer people weren't getting enough vitamins through not eating the right foods. In my dream I initiated a free fruit and veg market. It then cut, like a film cut, to the opening ceremony. I stood there like Lady Bountiful, thinking how nice to see everyone getting free fruit and veg. Cut again, this time to a huge mound of white button mushrooms. I opened my handbag, took out masses of plastic bags and starting filling the bags muttering to myself, '*They* won't appreciate these. They're mine!' I woke up in a terrible state,

thinking, 'That's what it's all about. It's just for *me*.' I had made
out it was for the benefit of poor people and in fact, it was because
I wanted a load of free mushrooms for myself!

There was another vivid dream during the 1960s where I told
the world that all the hippies were my friends and we understood
each other, I loved them and they were welcome in my home
any time. Then the dream cut to me sitting in the lotus position
on a sheepskin rug in the middle of my immaculate studio, with
all these hippies peeing over all my paintings — muck everywhere
— and I'm just sitting there smiling, saying, 'They are my friends.
I love them. But . . . why don't they clear off!' I woke up thinking,
'God! You're just a big load of shit.'

Who am I doing all this for? I suppose it's my compulsive
emotional response and my passionate desire to fight injustice
of any kind. I'd never campaign unless I felt strongly and could
do something effective, though. I have a burning sense of justice
which I inherited from my father, and I feel there is more injustice
now, at this particular time, than since the 1930s and the rise of
Moseley here and Hitler in Germany.

My father campaigned vociferously against Moseley. In fact,
our family was in Hitler's black book. I've a photocopy of the
entry with his name, Harry Samuels, the chambers' address, the
names of his wife and children, and our home address. Had Hitler
ever got here, we would have been amongst those to go to the
gas chambers. In a peculiar way I'm proud of that entry, and the
way my father spoke out against the Nazis. I can remember him
heckling the Moseleyites on Hampstead Heath. He articulated a
pertinent point and the lout on his orange box evaded the answer
shouting, 'Shut up, you dirty Jew!' I was six years old; it left such
a deep memory.

When the Anti-Nazi League was formed, I was asked to join
and became an active member of the steering committee. This
made me the subject of a certain amount of criticism from some
quarters of my own people — Jews — purely on the grounds
I was associating with a well-known anti-Zionist, Peter Hain. I
had to explain that Israel didn't enter into this particular campaign
because we were fighting racism, and surely we should all have
been fighting that, and it's possible to be bedfellows with someone
on one issue, and at odds with them on another, like Enoch Powell
and Tony Benn over the Common Market.

I think racism is unconsciously inherent in practically everyone.
Anyone who says they aren't racist is a liar. But a lot of

people work very hard at not being racist. To me, with some of
my mother's family ending their lives in the gas chambers, the
idea of being racist is obscene.

The depth of covert racism in my own profession frightens
me. It's rife among the casting directors who can't see beyond
the need for a black actor. Black actors are employed first for their
colour, second for their talent. I'm the token, white Jewish woman
on the Afro-Asian committee of Equity, and we've been fighting
for integrated casting for years to stop tokenism and stereotyping.

On the subject of Equity, I've opposed its policy on control
of entry into the profession. It's so frustrating for young people,
after three years at an accredited drama school, to be greeted by
a union which bars its doors and makes it impossible for them
to even go and audition. There are also a huge number of talented
people without any formal drama training, who should at least
be given the opportunity to audition, and if good enough, offered
a part. Why should they be denied union membership? That's
how it was in my day and I fail to see why it shouldn't be different
now.

I'm a founder member of Arts for Labour and believe the arts
policy of the next Labour government should include statutory
provision for theatre-in-education companies to visit every school
throughout the United Kingdom as part of the curriculum. That
way kids from families not theatre orientated will more easily and
naturally understand and appreciate the arts. I've never learned
to ski or drive or horse-ride, so when people talk about skiing,
or their cars, or horse-riding, it's beyond my experience. I don't
know what they're on about, and conversations about cars are
especially boring. It's all part of improving the quality of life, and
unless the opportunity is given to the young, they'll go to the
grave without the joy of ever having gone to a theatre or an art
gallery.

Lately, I've found I've an overactive thyroid, so now I say it's
not me that's campaigning, it's my thyroid — or rather me *and*
my thyroid. There're two of us at it!

Have you had to make any sacrifices and how do you feel about making them?

Yes. Not having children was a huge sacrifice. But, it would have
been impossible with my background, not having found anyone
I particularly wanted to marry, to have any children without

upsetting my parents. So, I suppose my campaigning is a sublimation for missing out on having a family and doing what every normal woman, which I am, should be doing.

Do you have difficulty making yourself and your own needs a top priority? How do you have fun and relax?

I used to have fun all the time — probably too much — so I avoid invitations if I think I've got to stand around in high heels all evening. I can't do it. I'm much happier going out to dinner somewhere with chums, where it's easy and cosy.

I haven't had a holiday since 1982, when I was with the RSC and we had the luxury of paid holidays. I went to Kenya alone and had the most wonderful time, and came back looking amazing and feeling glorious. Normally, when I'm working I can't spare the time, and if I'm not working I can't afford one, because I never save a penny. But that's another one of my problems!

Maybe after six months in this play, I'll take myself off again to be in the sun.

The most pleasurable times I've had have been in Australia. I've worked there a lot. Every weekend during the TV series, I used to take off for the beach just to splash about in the surf. All my worries disappear. There's nothing so healing for mind and body as the surf. I'd love to live by the sea.

Is it difficult keeping your private and public lives separate?

I've got such a boring private life at the moment that there's nothing to keep secret! Before, I managed pretty well to keep my private life private. The truth is, I'm not clever enough to have adopted a public persona. I don't know how to do it and I can't be bothered now.

Have you had to face failure and if so, what happened?

I'm pretty resilient. I can be in the depths of despair and contemplating suicide one minute, and the next I'll draw on my inherited Mother Courage indomitable spirit, and bounce back.

What have been your highest and lowest moments?

I've had quite a few high moments, professionally. There have been half a dozen really satisfying performances: *Mother Courage* (I played Helene Hanff and received the *Evening News* award); *Fiddler on the Roof*, in the production at Her Majesty's with Topol. I got a big buzz from that — it was such a success and we had so much fun doing it.

More recently, playing Anthony Sher's mother in *Torch Song Trilogy*. He managed to make me recapture the joys of being in theatre. I'd become a little jaded and wasn't liking myself very much, and working with Anthony was a rebirth. Going on stage every night was a total joy. I've practically adopted him as my son. It's wonderful to have such a relationship on and off stage. Being with someone you tremendously respect can only be stimulating.

Three plays by Saul Bellow were hugely successful and wonderful for me. They were two-handers with Harry Towb. I played three different desperate American females. We got rave reviews from the really intelligent critics. Bellow is a brilliant writer and his work is always taken seriously.

The mid-sixties were the best time for me. As well as *The Rag Trade*, I did *Fings Ain't Wot They Used to Be*, and got to know Noel Coward quite well, which I cherish enormously. It was the glimmerings of an egalitarian society, which has all but disintegrated now. I've talked about my regret at not having children, but in a way, another part of me says, 'Thank God I haven't got grandchildren, because I couldn't bear for them to grow up in this world.' We are handing them something so dreadful — the dismantling of many things that made us proud to be British, like the health service. I remember paying my first national health stamp at the end of July, 1948. We were the envy of the world. Aneurin Bevan had this dream and it came to fruition. I remember his wife, Jenny Lee, the Fairy Godmother of the arts, initiating the Arts Council. It was wonderful! Now, it's all disappearing. We talk in terms of private sponsorship and business, money, shares. Our public services, education, the things we hold dear, are all disintegrating.

I've tried to analyse why Mrs Thatcher is the way she is. We both grew up when ration books were our lifeline. Butter, cheese, meat, clothing were all rationed. People were very possessive

about their coupons. Our family had other priorities, in that as
well as being concerned about food and clothing, we were also
worried about being bombed, and what might have happened
to some of my mother's family in occupied Holland. A grocer's
daughter, Mrs Thatcher has retained that ration book mentality,
she's just substituted share ownership for food and clothing.

And your lowest moments?

At one time, when I was acting in *The Diary of Anne Frank*, I
went through a deep depression. It was in the 1950s. I took the
part, and the play, very personally. I thought some of my mother's
family didn't survive two-and-a-half years, so the least I could do
was live through two-and-a-half hours every night.

I thought I had cancer of the womb, everything. A very
perceptive stage manager saw what was happening to me, and
sent me to St Thomas's. I thought I was seeing a gynaecologist,
and couldn't understand why he didn't examine me. He never
said anything, and I never said anything. Then one week he said,
'I've done some television work myself, on my speciality, the hurt
mind.' I said, 'What! Is that what's wrong with me?'

'Just a little case of manic depression, dear.'

'Is that all?' I said. 'I know all about that. My father's had two
nervous breakdowns.' That got him scribbling away, at last he
had a behaviour pattern to work on! He turned out to be an
eminent psychiatrist, specializing in 'conditioning' problems. He
was awful. He put me on so many drugs I almost became a drug
addict. I realized I had to help myself, and it was yoga that got
me off the pills. Then, unfortunately, I had an operation on my
spine and couldn't do yoga anymore.

That was a very, very low period. I went through bizarre, mind-
blowing rituals. I could come home from the theatre, make some
food and hear voices telling me I had to have washed up by the
time I'd counted ten, or I had to put my shoes in a special spot,
otherwise I'd get a phone call saying my mother was dead. It was
terrible.

When do you feel most vulnerable?

Before first nights. I'm just terrified I'm going to be a failure, or
that I'm not going to feel right in the part. There's a very thin
dividing line. Even though you've got a performance locked in

your mind, you know who you are and what you're doing. Someone says the wrong thing and you've lost it, whereas someone saying the right thing at the right time and you take off.

The person who did that for me was Joan Littlewood. I was able to go through the first night of *Fings Ain't Wot They Used To Be* and actually enjoy every single moment. She was a great psychologist, she knew I had a good performance in me, but nerves could kill me. I might do too much and go over the top. She wanted me to be still and enjoy it. She sat in my dressing room for an hour before the curtain went up saying, 'God, you're a genius. You make me sick you're so good. The others all have to work hard, you don't have to, you can just stand there. It's so easy for you.' At the five minute call, I was like a racehorse — I couldn't wait to get on stage.

Moving house makes me feel very vulnerable. I'm typically Cancerian. I need order in my chaos, and all my possessions tidily around me. It's a problem, because I also long to be a slut, and be able to work even if the place is in a mess.

What are you most proud of?

My one-woman show about Liselotte, the Duchess of Orleans, Elisabeth Charlotte of Hanover, who was married off to Louis XIVs gay brother, the Duke of Orleans. They were known as Monsieur and Madame.

She was a very plain German girl, and at 19 her father was terrified she'd never marry, so he married her off to Monsieur, who had already been married before. She converted to Catholicism, lived at the Palace of Versailles and was a compulsive letter writer. She wrote copious letters and diaries about all the goings on in the court to all her aged German aunts, and her nurses, and so on. She wrote graphically about everyone farting, and all the other intimate details of court antics. She was appalled by it all. A virgin when she arrived, her first sexual experience was with a gay man who was surrounded by all his lovers. They somehow managed to have three children, and she says, 'After the birth of my third daughter in 1676, he left my bed and I never enjoyed ze business sufficiently to ask him to return.' Ze business was sex!

A talented writer, Maria Kroll, translated many of Liselotte's letters and the BBC asked me to do some Liselotte letter readings for Radio 3. I knew nothing about Lise at that stage, but I did the readings, which went down very well and I found myself becoming more and more intrigued by this woman. I bought a copy of the book of letters and then I did the most sensible thing I've ever done — asked father to lend me the money to buy the rights of the book, which he did.

Despite my manic exterior I'm very lazy; things often get pushed to one side. So I sat on them and did nothing for a long time, until my Dad said, 'I didn't give you the money to waste. Get on and do something with it.' So, I got off my bum, found a writer to dramatize the letters — Frederick Bradnum — and asked a young director — Peter Watson — who I was working with at the time, if he'd be interested in working on the project. He was delighted, and we worked together every day for three months, until the first airing at the Theatre Royal, York. It was an immediate success, and I've now done the show on the Fringe at the Edinburgh Festival, the Adelaide Festival, Melbourne, the Phoenix theatre in London, and several university theatres. But the biggest success of all was in Vienna at the English-speaking theatre.

It was incredible — they didn't know me from a bar of soap, but they knew the character. Here, it was the other way round; they knew me, but not the character. They thought it remarkable that an English actress should bring them their own palatinate princess. It was a tremendous success.

Once in a while I do it again. It's an interesting part to play because there are always extra dimensions to bring to the character.

It was about that time, 1975, I got my OBE. The day of the investiture was my first night doing the Liselotte show in Brighton. I was doubly nervous: not only was I meeting the Queen, but I was terrified I'd trip while curtseying and afraid I'd miss my one o'clock Brighton train from Victoria. At 12.15 it was my turn. Of course you are told about the protocol: she may talk to you, she may not, but *you* don't initiate a conversation. In fact, she did speak to me.

'I'm so happy to be giving you this. Are you working at the moment?' And I said, 'Yes, Ma'am, I'm opening tonight in Brighton, playing one of Your Majesty's relatives.' She looked rather taken aback, and probably thought it was a ghastly send-up of Princess Margaret or something, so I went on quickly, '. . . Elisabeth Charlotte of Hanover.' What I would have liked to say was '. . . Elisabeth Charlotte of Hanover, and I'm so happy Your Majesty lives near Victoria station!'

I'm proud of my extraordinarily good ear for accents and dialects, which, strangely enough, after 42 years in the business is only now being appreciated and exploited.

Can you tell me some of the people you've admired?

When I began in the business, the woman I regarded as my fairy godmother was Sybil Thorndike. She was wonderful to me, and got me my first job. She acted with us in our last term at RADA, playing Marmie in *Little Women*. I was stage managing and playing Aunt March as well. I'm very much a perfectionist as far as props are concerned, and Marmie receives a cablegram, so I made sure it was the right kind and stuck down properly — so well, in fact, that Sybil Thorndike couldn't open it! I was mortified. Anyway, she forgave me and subsequently said I should contact her after RADA.

When I finished, she was doing a very heavy season at the New (now the Alberry) theatre with Laurence Olivier, Ralph Richardson and her old man, Sir Lewis Casson, and I boldly dropped her a note asking to see her after the matinee. She was wonderful, saw me and wrote her husband a note of introduction, and he gave me a job — understudy to his daughter Ann in St Joan.

Sybil became my idol. I admire her so much as a woman. She was, to my mind, the paragon, because she was never frightened to speak out, and that's what I liked. It was through her I became interested in Equity, the actors' union, because she and Sir Lewis were both very active and regarded as leftist at the time. She had her regimented life irrespective of anything. Every morning she used to practice an hour of Bach at the piano, learn a Greek stanza of verse every day to keep the brain juice flowing and the memory cells oiled. I often wonder why I don't do the same!

Latterly, my idol, and I think I can honestly say a friend, is Peggy Ashcroft. To me, she epitomizes the best of womanhood and the theatre. She will stand up and be counted on important issues. I admire her integrity and her beauty. She is extraordinary, in that although she is a great star, she makes you feel she's an ordinary woman. I've left it a bit late now, but if there is someone I wish to emulate, it's Peggy. I think she's the most consummate actress. She's always been brilliant, but she somehow seems to improve with age!

Dame Peggy Ashcroft.
Reproduced courtesy of
Hulton Picture Library.

Sybil Thorndyke.
Reproduced courtesy of
Hulton Picture Library.

Do you have a sense of your own spirituality?

I would like to be able to answer 'Yes,' but I think that sounds
terribly smug and conceited. I'm here one minute, then I'm gone.
Life is so ephemeral. When I'm gone, I expect my friends will
say, 'Poor old Mim. Pity, she was quite good really. She meant
well. She did shoot her mouth off an awful lot . . .' And that'll
be that. What there is on the other side I know not, but there
obviously is something, because I'm tremendously psychic. So
I can't disregard the fact there are some things about which we
are ignorant.

How do you know you're psychic?

I have extraordinary, often very traumatic, forecasting dreams and
I can't account for the fact I dream so accurately prior to something
happening. It's so weird — they always follow the same pattern.
I wake up in a sweat, sitting bolt upright, not knowing what to
do about it, yet knowing it's definitely going to happen.

I dreamed about an air crash at Gatwick three hours before
it happened, and once, in Australia, I awoke hysterical because
I'd dreamed about a car pile-up on Piermont bridge, Sydney. The
next morning I told three people about it and asked if they thought
I should tell the authorities. One said, 'No. Just don't *you* go across
the bridge.' Another patted my head and took no notice. I went
to rehearsal and afterwards one of the friends I'd told rang, saying
it had been on the news: a terrible car crash with one vehicle
hanging over the edge, exactly as I'd dreamed.

I dreamed about my own burglary the night before it happened,
even to the light bulb blowing. I had a secret switch outside my
bedroom door which lit the entire studio, and in my dream it
failed. Next day, I discovered all the electricity had gone
throughout the house. That evening I came home, heard a thud
upstairs, went up to have a look, and there at the window was
the burglar.

What lessons have you learned?

My friends would probably say, 'She's obviously learned bugger
all!' I keep repeating my mistakes; the premise is often different,
but I find myself reacting in more or less the same way.

The one thing I *have* learned is not to throw tantrums every five minutes. I'm not sure I'm any calmer inside; I still feel very turbulent. But now when I raise my voice, it's usually because something very important has gone wrong. I used to be an hysteric and I'm not any more.

What's your personal vision?

I know it's naive of me, but I do actually believe in universal Utopian socialism, a brotherhood of man. To me, one of the most moving things to happen recently was Bob Geldof initiating Band Aid and achieving the impossible: he managed to make people all over the world care about one single issue and brought them together for a common cause. I would to God I could emulate him.

For instance, I'm the patron of London Entertains, which organizes a multi-cultural, multi-racial festival annually. Two years ago, I compered the event and at the end I was so excited after seeing performers from Britain as well as Swedes, Estonians, Germans, ordinary Asian women from Southall dancing, Africans, the north, south and central Americans, I leapt on to the podium and said, 'Wouldn't it be wonderful if everyone here went back home and organized the same event in their own city, and on the same day, at the same time, we could celebrate our different cultures together all over Britain.' Who knows, perhaps eventually we could organize it annually, worldwide. I know it won't happen in the same way as Band Aid; local politics and politicians will get in the way. But I wanted everyone to think about the idea seriously and try to do something.

I have felt for a long time now how marvellous it would be if, on a given day at a given time, everybody everywhere in the world would stop fighting and put their hatred of each other to one side.